Perfect
Dealership

SURVIVING THE DIGITAL
DISRUPTION

Max Zanan

ISBN: 1977545513

ISBN-13: 9781977545510

Library of Congress Control Number: 2017915550

CreateSpace Independent Publishing Platform

North Charleston, South Carolina

Table of Contents

Preface

My work as a professional consultant for *all aspects* of the auto dealership demands foresight. Without it, I could not do my job well, and what I now see is the following: there is a paradigm shift underway in the auto sales and service business. The older business model that made many of us a good living is now being replaced, yet most of the general managers, dealer principals, and others I do consulting for do not see this. These changes have already begun, but the veterans in this business remain in the dark. Only those who understand what is happening will take over the market share. In response to these changing conditions, I have written this book, which is unlike any other I am aware of. With *Perfect Dealership*, I want to offer the general managers, dealer principals, and others in our business an understanding of why such perfection is now necessary. I also want to provide a concrete plan for achieving this transformation.

Intelligence means, among other things, the ability to see the changes coming your way and to adapt to them—to understand the actualities in front of you and react in time. So far, only a handful of newcomers see these openings, and they have already moved to exploit them. Vroom represents the new model as well as any company out there. You would be hard-pressed to find a single dealership in America lately that has raised $10 million in investment capital, but Vroom has raised over $200 million in in the last few years. Vroom, Carvana, Shift, and a few other new companies specialize in used car sales on the Internet, where the showroom is a website. The product is late-model used cars of quality. The catch is brutally simple: "Try the car for a week or for up to a thousand miles. If you like it, keep it. If not, return it at no charge." We can examine Vroom in more detail later, but the seemingly simple business model has initiated a fateful paradigm shift in the used-car market, which will never be the same again. I repeat: Vroom *initiated* the shift, because what began in the used market will spread to all areas, including new cars, finance and insurance (F&I), and fixed operations.

At work here, underneath the top layer of an Internet business, is a fundamental principle: "Give the customer the tools to buy a car how he or she wants to, and support the process with the best-informed and best-trained staff you can develop." *Develop,* not hire or find. *Careful development* is another key, because our business has been operating in an ad hoc manner for too long. Creating the Perfect Dealership requires an understanding of all this, and of fundamentals that I have been pushing for years, like the principle that the whole is larger than the sum of the parts.

Your departments must function like a Swiss watch, where the parts are all interconnected and not de facto operating separately from one another. When one moves, the others are informed, and the assumption is that there is a common goal. In the dealership, all departments must work toward a common goal. In its simplest form, that goal should be this: customer satisfaction, which ensures customer retention. Sales needs to be a career commensurate with other respected careers, not a gig that has a high turnover. Offer people a career, not a job with high turnover. Training and support must be there for the new hires, and they must have the concrete opportunity to develop and rise to the level of their innate ability. We must support a solid future for our employees, because this is what the good ones want, and they also help us make our living.

Information technology (IT) has changed, and software is essential for the smooth functioning of day-to-day operations. This must also be addressed to create the Perfect Dealership. Related to this is the 24-7 world we now live in, where quickness of response will separate the winners from the losers. We will look into this. And we need to remember that car sales is a local phenomenon. Be active in the community, and take a genuine interest in the lives of your customers. Then, when they pass the dealership on the road, they will gladly turn in and do business with you. Become an asset for a man or woman raising a family inside a community, and you may well have a loyal customer for life. The fundamentals will always apply.

But it is crucial change that is blindsiding us, so we will never get a chance to improve those fundamentals. Don't let a Vroom alone blaze the path that you should have forged: Used car sales on the Internet leads to a broad, trusting customer base, and before you know it, Toyota grants Vroom a dealership. They brand their name in all areas and develop F&I products. Their service departments pop up all over the country, and everywhere they are trusted by their customers. Then, eventually they are selling parts, and it is game over. Amazon buys them out—and where are you?

Better yet Amazon buys AutoNation (the largest publicly held auto group in the country) similar to the way they acquired Whole

Foods. Overnight Amazon will have 330 physical locations across the country. Amazon is willing to work on extremely low margins, they basically invented e-commerce, understand logistics, and have consumers' trust. Let that sink in for a moment.

This book is a wake-up call. The Perfect Dealership will address these topics and more. My goal in this book is to make all of us better and to bring respect to our business by aspiring to excellence—in all *interconnected* operations. I see no reason why this cannot happen, soon. Failure to adopt and change will result in the disappearance of the existing brick and mortar dealership model. Car dealership might be the next corner video store and travel agency.

Chapter One

Why I Wrote This Book

What, then, makes for the Perfect Dealership? What are the primary obsessions that lead to perfection? I use the word *obsession* in the positive sense, because without it you'll be left far behind by others who *are* obsessed and who feel compelled to learn, act, and continually do better in the more difficult, competitive climate we're entering.

The following are all equally critical to our business. All will lead to excellence:

- obsession with customer service
- obsession with employee training
- obsession with product knowledge
- a shared, common goal among all departments

Obsessed with Customer Service

"Customer service is not a department; it is a philosophy" is a quote attributed to Steve Jobs. Apple has just a few products, all centered on the personal computer, and it has a focus on the customer that is second to none.

With this in mind, I walked into their flagship store in Manhattan and found a manager on the sales floor. I asked, "Who do you want to see apply for a job at Apple?" He told me the following:

"Anyone could apply for work here as a salesperson. What I mean is that you don't need to have expertise in computers. We'll train for that. What we look for first is a modicum of intelligence, so the person can get the expertise, but what we really prize is strong social skills. Apple realizes that sales is the front line, that it is all about what type of person you put out on the floor for the customers that walk in the door.

"The salesperson who is sensitive to the importance and needs of the client is the better choice. These are extremely technical products, and the techs have their departments, and obviously they are absolutely essential to the business. But, you know, the detached, inward, introverted personality would be better off working on the machines away from the sales floor.

"We're talking about sales as the front line, so it's the person who can approach the client with the ability to listen and react in a very helpful way, and eventually anticipate those needs, that is valued above someone who already has the IT expertise but is without the necessary people skills. Again, there are other departments better suited to the tech-minded person with an inward personality. We need sharp, reactive, social types on the floor making the sales and retaining customers. We need intermediary-type per-sonalities weighted toward the technical on the Genius Bar for repairs and tweaks. The customers need the best people for each kind of job, and we see to that. But customer service is everything here. Without it," he smiled, "we would not be Apple."

And this is exactly what I experienced in the store. Every employee was either focused and engaged with a customer or waiting eager-ly, projecting an attitude of deference to be of help. I talked to sev-eral staff members, and all my questions were answered in detail. When I threw in a more obscure question about a legacy computer, I was led to a manager and scheduled to talk to a "genius" in a few minutes (the "genius" thing is annoying, granted; it undervalues a Stephen Hawking), and every attempt was made to inform me on exactly what I wanted to know. The whole experience was positive, and never did I feel that I knew more than they did, as a collective.

Another company that leaps out from the pack is Costco, which is gaining more market share every year against Walmart and other competitors. I had an informative meeting once with someone who had launched a top-tier credit card (that focused on extraor-dinary customer service and made popular the term "privilege") at a time when the business was ripe for innovation. He is a thought leader in the business and a top CEO.

We got on the subject of successful businesses seen as proto-types, and he told me he admired Costco. He had recently gone into one of their stores and had a great experience. In walking around and catching the feel and flow of their operations on the shopping floor, he was struck by the focus and positive energy of the employees, to the point where he wanted to talk to a few of them and hear their thoughts. What he found was a group of people who felt well respected, well trained, well remunerated, and carefully listened to. Here was a company that respects its hires and provides for their training, development, and well-being.

I am writing this book mainly for dealer principals and general managers. Imagine the effect of such a sales force on customers, with such a winning combination of attributes. This is what leads to sales, above all else. We're dealing with a public that is increasingly sophisticated about our products, and they need to have a reason to come to our dealerships.

Customer retention will be the new benchmark for how you are doing. Retention should be the focus. If you are excellent enough to retain your customer base, it will clearly help you acquire new ones. That is, retaining customers due to excellence at a Perfect Dealership will lead—by word of mouth, Internet reviews, and other referral methods—to new buyers and increased profits.

Employee Training
So, what makes great customer service? We've already mentioned training, but let's focus on it in this section.

First of all, great employees are made by great training; otherwise, management is not doing its job.

The value of training should be self-evident. Olympic athletes train, scientists train, as do mechanics, concert pianists, doctors, lawyers, artists, and technicians in all fields. In fact, the training for most professional fields is extensive.

Anything that produces work of lasting value takes time and effort and probably has a recognizable standard. Some of these standards are imposed and regulated by professional associations that demand a license. Medicine, for example, demands four years of premed in college, four more of medical school, then a year of internship, and, finally, three years of residency. And *then* you get your doctor's license only by passing a state exam.

An auto mechanic's training would typically be less extensive than, say, a surgeon's to get started in the field, but an experienced professional is always valued. *Work* is the real education at the end of the day.

Big IT companies develop sophisticated cultures. Microsoft and Google are on the extreme end and actually design entire communities for their workers—villages that have their own transportation and infrastructure. They want their workers bound together in a constant interaction so that they share experiences and ideas. This includes training and lectures and a full indoctrination into the core ideas and values of their businesses. How carefully an employee is watched and guided at these companies is not hard to imagine. Training happens at the start of these careers, but it is an ongoing process.

OK, so not all of us have the resources of these giants. But what about auto sales and service and the fact that, too often, there is a *total lack of any training at all?* The difficulty of achieving one extreme (the excellence demonstrated by the best companies that can easily afford this attainment) should not justify the other extreme: total neglect.

Most new hires in the auto business begin almost immediately, and there is little, if any, training available other than to watch and question more experienced colleagues. This is how bad habits carry over from one generation to the next.

I contend these days are over. The level of service and expertise we now need to offer will demand good training programs.
The investment will keep you alive and may even allow you to
thrive.

In principle, *strategy needs to be longer term.* This is a luxury if
you are struggling, granted, and are fixed on making your bottom
line for the short term. But for many dealerships, it is more a matter of realizing that training instills excellence and is *necessary.*
When something is deemed to be necessary then we act on it
and no longer neglect it. Things believed to be optional easily get
delayed or forgotten.

Don't wait until you are hemorrhaging profits to set up a training
program that prepares employees in advance so that when they
are ready to work, they are an asset to the business and don't
come off as a liability.

Effective training should have a positive effect on business goals
and objectives. A perfect example of successful training is Jiffy
Lube. Yes, Jiffy Lube. Training at Jiffy Lube is responsible for reduced employee turnover, eight consecutive years of increased
average revenue per customer, and improved customer service
scores. Take a look at the statistics below, and I guarantee you
will have a crystal-clear understanding of the importance of
training:

- total number of Jiffy Lube International, Inc., employees
  and service center employees trained overall annually:
  20,000
- average length of employee service: 12 years

- percentage of job openings filled by internal candidates: 90 percent
- percentage of new hires referred by employees: approximately 80 percent
- total number of employees and independent contractors/franchisees trained annually via instructor-led classroom sessions: 3,000
- total number of employees and independent contractors/franchisees trained annually via online, self-paced study: 20,000
- number of courses offered as instructor-led classroom sessions: 9
- number of courses offered as instructor-led virtual classroom sessions: 4
- number of courses offered as online-self-paced modules: 120
- total hours of training taken in 2013: 2.2 million

I am yet to see a dealership that does a fraction of Jiffy Lube's educational/training output.

For our auto business, training needs to center on examining techniques and ways of communicating on the sales floor, and also—and this brings us to our next focus—on striving for perfect product knowledge.

Investment to date in training by serious companies is about $165 billion. The average investment per worker last year went up to just under $1,800, up from $1,200 in 2012.

♦ ♦ ♦

Properly explaining how to effectively train employees requires, in itself, a whole book, but let me put these ideas in your head:

- Where is not as important as what. Whether you offer on-site courses, online courses, or live webinars, the main consideration is that content is king.
- One approach is to be very focused and align each course with a single goal. Choose one desired result. Make one leader—a person in the dealership—accountable for that course.
- Have a company philosophy that is more important than any other short-term expedient. (Hewlett Packard comes to mind here—look up their history and the specific corporate culture they developed.)
- Have a means of following up the results of the training. Periodic income will, of course, be a measure.
- Training costs money and takes away from employee time on the sales floor or in the shop. Still, average investment at good companies is up now from thirty hours a year to about fifty-seven. This is one good reason why they lead in their fields. I have yet to see a dealership where employees spend fifty-seven hours per year training.

Accept all these fundamental points as *necessary*—not as optional. In other words, we are offering a career to our employees, not a gig, and will train them to develop a business culture that has at its center a ladder of upward mobility for the best people. And all of this will contribute to our ROI (return on investment) by yielding positive growth.

I urge you to invest and set-up in extensive training programs now while the sales are strong and most dealerships are profitable. It will be much harder, if not impossible, to do so during the next downturn.

Obsessed with Product Knowledge

Let me preface these remarks with a brief story. I wanted a 4Runner Limited last year and decided I would like ventilated seats. I entered the dealership and began asking about this. Everything I was told was wrong: "They don't exist," "I'm not sure; let me check," "No, they don't make these," and so forth. So I got online and did the research myself. As I expected, they do exist in the Limited model. I went back to the dealership, but again I was told that they do not exist.

I bought the car anyway, and guess what—heated seats and ventilated seats are controlled by the same knob. Let this sink in for a minute. The only thing that a salesperson had to do was to sit in the car and make a minimal effort.

Imagine my impression of this dealership and whether I will go back there for repairs. Why the hell do I need this kind of incompetence?

There has to be a good reason to walk onto your sales floor, and ignorance is not that reason. In a Perfect Dealership, your sales staff must know every minute detail about every car and every package available. Thorough product knowledge will always help close more deals. Customers must know that your dealership is the place where they can get the very best information for making their best purchase.

The Internet is here to stay. Information is readily available on any new or used product, no matter how detailed is the information you seek. Consumers are becoming more and more educated because of an increasing number of online sources for researching their next car.

Therefore, it is not uncommon—in fact, it is becoming closer to the norm—for the customer to walk into the showroom and know more about the car than the sales staff or managers. This is unacceptable.

Salespeople should be required to attain certification for each model they sell, and neither salespeople nor sales managers should be allowed on the floor without certification. When was the last time your dealership had a walk-around competition? When this level of training becomes your norm, then you can say management deserves respect.

All Departments Must Have a Common Goal

The general manager together with the service and parts director, the finance director, and the BDC (Business Development Center) manager must work together to design a perfect customer experience.

Many times when I consult car dealers, I see that sales, fixed ops, and the F&I department are run almost independently of one another. Instead, they need to work together and act as a force multiplier on one another. This will further boost customer experience.

For example, customer experience in the service department (wait time, comfort, ease of making an appointment, and so forth) may well determine whether or not the customer will buy his or her next car from that dealership. It will help determine brand loyalty as the customer associates the purchased product with the quality of the operation that services it.

Ideas bind people. A Perfect Dealership must have a mission statement that is clearly articulated, and all departments and their employees must work toward it. And don't keep it a secret—display your mission statement in the showroom and your website. This will only make customers more comfortable. This is a crucial point. Nothing is more impressive than an operation where everything feels like a part of everything else it works with. A familiar image would be when a racecar makes a pit stop at Daytona, and everyone attends to the car and driver. Everyone and everything connected to that car works to win the race, just as working together at a dealership moves the totality of the operation forward.

By the same token, nothing is more mediocre than an operation where everyone is out for him- or herself. The customer feels it, and the employees feel it and react to one another's indifference or self-serving behavior, often making it worse.

Management is the place for this unity to begin and spread from the top down.

◆ ◆ ◆

The main point here is this: an ad hoc approach to hiring and developing is detrimental to success and should be avoided at all costs, especially as profit margins will get tighter moving forward.

Solid training, of course, is part of the answer. It is an up-front cost, at least at first, and so is too often avoided.

But the career itself requires structural changes so that who you can train improves. The people who apply need to be at a level where the training is worth the cost. Again, better hires want the option of a career, not a gig or an improvised operation where they live by their wits. It is axiomatic that if you are truly offering a career to your employees, you have created a solid business that has depth.

◆ ◆ ◆

Let me finish this chapter by pointing out to you the main obstacles to getting the better staff you need as you aspire to put together the Perfect Dealership:

The following shortcomings apply to almost every dealership I have ever worked in or studied, until I made an effort to change them:

- long hours (twelve hours per day is typical)
- lack of training (everything is done ad hoc, on the fly)
- commission-based pay (making it hard to survive while getting started in the new career)

These three problems are paramount, though of course there are others. As a result, dealerships cannot and do not even try to hire college graduates. The "sink or swim" structure of the business means a salesperson either makes it or doesn't. Primarily because of this, dealerships can fail; however, mostly, too many salespeople never realize their full potential.

Dealerships, in short, need to make auto sales into a viable career through which the salespeople can develop and grow and find security and stability—just like someone who chooses to go into banking, government, or health care.

But, to date, dealerships are not offering the new hire much in the way of a normal career. Certainly, too many of us in the industry have yet to offer a career that can be developed in a structured way with solid support so that our staff, the lifeblood of any operation, is not fighting an uphill battle.

Chapter Two

Who Should Read This Book

This is a short chapter to clarify who this book was written for. *Perfect Dealership* is intended mainly for dealer principals. Importantly, it also targets their general managers, many of whom aspire to be owners someday. It welcomes the industrious newcomer as well, and it should benefit *anyone* seeking a career in the auto field.

To Dealer Principals

Our business has so far defied a law of nature: the law of the conservation of energy. This normally means that business consolidates in the direction of power. The bigger corporations buy out the ones underneath them so that everything consolidates over time. In the IT world it is easy to spot the winners: Google, Intel, Microsoft, Sun, Oracle, and so forth.

But in auto retail you still have a fragmented world of dealerships owned by individual dealer principals. This is now changing and will succumb to the consolidative forces and economy-of-scale principle that will soon start to overwhelm the industry. If you own a traditional dealer principal business, this is another wake-up call.

Recent examples of powerful consolidating interests include AutoNation, Group-1, and Warren Buffet's acquisition of Van Tuyl Auto Group, and this is only the beginning. There are private equity firms buying dealerships like drunken sailors. The driving force of this new trend is clear, and, again, in order for you to survive this new market development, you will need to run your dealership like a fine Swiss watch.

Here is the start of a *Forbes* article about Buffet's March 2015 acquisition:

> NEW YORK—Investment guru Warren Buffett and the auto retail industry had a lot of nice things to say about each other at an auto conference today.
>
> "It's a huge industry. It can be, if run properly, a very good business," said Buffett, chairman and CEO of Omaha-based Berkshire Hathaway Inc.
>
> The mutual admiration society was no surprise. Buffet closed a deal earlier this month to buy the nation's largest, privately held auto dealership chain, the Phoenix-based Van Tuyl Group, the fourth-largest auto retail chain in the United States based on 2014 new-vehicle retail unit sales of 139,538, according to Automotive News.

The move was Buffett's first acquisition in auto retailing, and it was seen as a big seal of approval for the auto retailing business model. Note his one comment of substance here: "It's a huge industry. It can be, if run properly, a very good business."

The article mentions the scale of the acquisition:

> The Van Tuyl Group, based in Phoenix, has 78 dealerships in 10 states, and annual sales of around $9 billion. The company was renamed Berkshire Hathaway Automotive, with headquarters in Dallas.

Note that managers retain equity in their respective dealership, a key feature of Van Tuyl's philosophy.

My point, however, is this: the consolidation that amounts to a natural law in the corporate arena has begun in our business. Excellence, and an understanding of the nature of the changes and how to adapt—as I will keep emphasizing—is the bulwark to survival.

The recent purchase of Whole Foods illustrates that Amazon is not opposed to going into brick-and-mortar businesses. Buying AutoNation or any other large player will not even put a dent in Amazon's finances.

To General Managers
This book is also meant for general managers. Those worth their salt will often aspire to be owners at some point. My first thought for the ambitious GM is this: It is critical that you work and move in step with your dealer principals, despite your ambition and self-directive tendencies. Those born to lead can easily take offense when things are not done as they believe they should be done.

When managing, you may make moves, whether fully intentional or not, that override your dealer principal. You may believe this is for the best and that your actions help profits. But I would urge all levels of management to unify. The downside of uncoordinated actions is worse than the potential upside.

So, get educated together on the coming changes, and agree on common goals. Otherwise, your potential and that of the dealership get lost in a scattering of resources, and you will then get people or whole departments working at odds with one another.

The principles in this book are carefully considered and sound, as well as prescient for the coming market and can be vetted in a relatively short amount of time: half a year to a year should show results. Owners ultimately have the final say, but it is important to have all management working in harmony. General managers must be 100 percent on board, or they should leave and do things their own way somewhere else.

Everyone will benefit when the entire team makes a concerted, unified effort toward the Perfect Dealership. The talented GM must learn to sell his or her strategies to the whole team. And we all know the dealership is only as good as the GM running it. If you must, leave and go your own way. But seek unity before fragmentation.

To Anyone Seeking a Career in Automotive Retail
To everyone else, especially newcomers, I welcome you into our business. A career in auto sales can be very rewarding. I'm a good example and have to look no further than myself and the opportunities I made use of to get where I am. Use this book as a first road map to illustrate what a great business this can be if done correctly, as Buffet remarked in the article above.

Chapter Three

Human Resources

Dealerships are sales organizations, so most consultants focus on sales. But this focus on sales is what got the industry into trouble in the first place. There is a lack of awareness of causal links in this sales-centric approach.

Attention instead should be on one critical question: Who will be representing the Perfect Dealership and selling our cars and how?

That can't be answered by hauling out a megaphone and yelling, "Go out on the floor and sell. These are the incentives!" This MO is typical of our field: we throw things at the wall and see what sticks, and we push and improvise at sales to see who has the talent as the revolving door turns and turns—instead of defining and refining the human resources that will bring us the money. We are caught way downstream of any real control, in other words.

Part of the responsibility for rushing to sales is our fault, but also partly to blame are the original equipment manufacturers (OEMs) that push dealers into a rat race. Because of this OEM-applied pressure, we end up chasing a sales quota all the time. Car business is the only business I know if that reports earnings/sales on a monthly basis. This approach has severe limitations, taking away from customer experience and contributing to customer dissatisfaction. Moreover, monthly reporting requirement destroys strategic thinking and long-term planning.

In an aspiring Perfect Dealership, we need to reorder our priorities. The first step is to focus on human resources and develop human capital, not simply to shove our employees onto a sales floor and see who can survive and then whether they want to stay.

Here is a principle: whatever gives you a long-term edge is what you should be doing. Anything that will help a dealership *adapt* in the midst of a paradigm shift—like the major one we are in now— will start to appear all over the place, sooner or later. (Again, don't be the last one to notice.)

It is worth restating this in a number of contexts:

- Human Resources is the new platform from which the dealership should be expanding its whole operation.

- Employee learning and development is a hot field right now, because business is getting more and more sophisticated and competitive.
- The message is getting clearer year by year: a planned and careful approach to the development of an educated, prepared staff (versus the old ad hoc approach) increases the quality of a dealership and, therefore, its profits.

Sadly, most dealerships *don't have* a dedicated HR director. Please let this sink in. Dealerships usually let a comptroller perform this function, as if that person had the specific training. The problem is that too many of us tend to focus on the narrow picture. Unfortunately, that's not enough. There is much more potential in developing human capital than just filing signed sexual harassment and workplace violence forms.

Perfect Dealerships need a dedicated person to create job descriptions, work out pay plans, hire, train, retain and fulfill all the roles trained HR staff do at successful companies. That is, a good HR person can *develop* human capital and provide policy and procedures as well as a training framework for new hires and existing staff.

Let's explore some of these functions using specifics:

Hiring the right person for any position at a dealership is critical. HR should look for someone who considers car sales a career, not a temporary gig before something better becomes available. These people will start to emerge more as we change and offer them more. In other words, we need to see that we're in a transitional period, and the more we develop ourselves as a business that offers permanence to its employees, the more educated, talented, articulate, and stable people will seek us out.

It is also mission critical to conduct background checks and verify references in order to make those good hiring decisions, and HR should pick up these duties. Another excellent tool to weed out bad apples is drug testing. I strongly suggest checking for prescription drugs in light of the current opioid epidemic in our country. In addition, checking credit should be part of the hiring process, as it is in other industries. Drug tests, credit checks, and asset checks should be done in case of promotion from within, as well.

At the same time, workloads must become equitable. HR should develop a forty-hour schedule for sales staff and managers to attract the higher-caliber applicants. This is becoming a necessity to attract quality personnel. Bell-to-bell hours are the biggest turnoff, especially to millennials. (If you don't think there's been a generational shift in attitude, think again. A tangential piece of advice here is to figure out how younger hires are different and how to influence them.)

In addition, a Perfect Dealership should offer a combination of a decent salary with commissions to reduce turnover. Existing primarily on commission is very stressful, and those of us who came up the old way know this firsthand. It takes a special kind of personality to endure this kind of financial pressure and thrive in it. Offer a better salary to reduce the pressure. If you have taken the trouble to put your new employees through a training program, they are already vetted and valuable in your eyes.

A related point: a bonus structure focused on customer satisfaction and retention instead of volume will drastically improve customer experience. Currently most dealers pay very little salary to salespeople, $100–$200 per week, augmented by a volume bonus on top of the commission. That places the emphasis on sales and not on the customer satisfaction that will drive future sales to new heights. (Thinking this way is intelligent using a long-term approach—rather than a fear-based, bottom-line oriented mentality. This is chess, not checkers. It is deceptively easy for a manager to retain this status quo mentality if he came up the hard way in the business—but ultimately this will hurt profits and, worse, chances of survival in the new environment.) Never forget that it is consumers' dissatisfaction with the current buying process that causes Silicon Valley to come up with new ways to disrupt our business. Keep this in mind: Autotrader surveyed 4000 people and asked if they were satisfied with the current selling process in the dealerships across the country. 17 people said "Yes". That's less than one percent!

Let's return to training for a moment (something we will do repeatedly, given its importance): Perfect Dealerships don't expect employees to pick up information and quality techniques by osmosis. HR needs to take over and train employees on a regular basis. Effective onboarding together with ongoing training is the key.

Currently, many salespeople are expected to talk to customers their first day on the floor. Think of this happening at an Apple store, for example, or at a Jiffy Lube, where training is made paramount. Or imagine an NFL team letting a new player into a game the same day they hire him. Think, generally, of how ludicrous this is. This practice emerged in a sales environment that used to more easily offer success, so perhaps it made sense, but that's no longer the case.

I'm telling you, these days are over.

The HR manager needs to be at the helm to develop a training program for employees in service, parts, body shop, BDC, F&I, and sales. And there must also be a training program for management and leadership. This is a big undertaking—I am only summarizing here, to get you pointed in the right directions— and the HR manager should work closely with state dealer association, which already provides a lot of training courses for its members.

So, to sum up, without training, success is limited, and thus training must exist at all levels. There is a need not only for sales training, but for leadership training as well. But with good leadership, this happens naturally.

We also need to pay attention to the ethics and compliance training for the entire organization. Unfortunately, dealers across the country do not have the best reputation. Integrating ethics, compliance, and antifraud programs into the dealership curriculum will improve customer experience and perception.

This will ultimately result in a transparent sales experience, and that is exactly what today's customer is craving. That transparent sales experience will translate into higher customer satisfaction and retention, referrals, and profits.

Upward Mobility inside the Dealership

With good employees properly trained, the Perfect Dealership must provide a path for newly hired salespeople, technicians, and managers to advance their careers through additional training and promotion. They have to know that, with good work, they have a chance to move up and get promoted.

Promotion is critical to long-term operations, depth, and stability. Promotion from within reduces turnover, contributes to continuity, and makes customers comfortable because they know that, when they come back, there are familiar faces, and they will receive the same great experience and service.

Currently, successful salespeople get promoted to sales managers or finance managers. Just because they were good at sales, it doesn't mean they will be any good at managing. The Perfect Dealership and its HR director should be looking for leadership qualities, not just sales numbers. Moreover, once a salesperson is promoted, additional training must be provided in order to ensure success.

As already explained, the best practice is to run a background check (criminal, credit, and asset check) again at the time of promotion to make sure that the candidate fits the criteria.

NADA and State Dealer Associations

Dealer principals should send its managers to NADA (National Automobile Dealers Association) conventions to look for the latest developments in the industry. NADA provides a wealth of online courses and webinars to its members. Also, NADA has an excellent university, and I strongly suggest that you send your future general managers and dealer principals to learn the business.

Yes, You Are All on a Mission
HR directors also must develop clear policies that outline expectations of employees. These should cover such areas as dress, drug/alcohol use, document falsification, sexual harassment, workplace violence, and the like.

To be sure the message gets across, HR directors must outline expectations, so each new employee realizes the handbook isn't just something to be signed and ignored. New hires must be tested on their understanding of what is expected of them.

A good HR director will have effective onboarding for hew hires and ongoing training for existing employees.

The Mission Statement
Every dealership must have a mission statement that every employee knows. A mission statement is intended to clarify the goals of the company. Here is an example from Nordstrom's, a large department store chain:

> Nordstrom's works relentlessly to give customers the most compelling shopping experience possible based on John Nordstrom's founding philosophy: Offer the customer the best possible service, selection, quality and value.

Most mission statements are just one sentence.

Here is Facebook's: "To give people the power to share and make the world more open and connected."

PayPal's: "To build the web's most convenient, secure, cost-effective payment solution."

Hewlett Packard is a well-known, classic example of a company run by a philosophy. It is well worth quoting in full here:

> The founders developed a management style that came to be known as "The HP Way."
>
> In Hewlett's words, the HP Way is "a core ideology... which includes a deep respect for the individual, a dedication to affordable quality and reliability, a commitment to community responsibility, and a view that the company exists to make technical contributions for the advancement and welfare of humanity."

The following are the tenets of The HP Way:

- We have trust and respect for individuals.
- We focus on a high level of achievement and contribution.
- We conduct our business with uncompromising integrity.
- We achieve our common objectives through teamwork.
- We encourage flexibility and innovation.

Develop your own mission statement. Display it proudly on the dealer's website as well as inside the dealership.

It is a good idea to not just develop a mission statement but to outline your corporate vision and core values.

Code of Ethics

A code of ethics is similar to a mission statement and must be displayed on the website and in the showroom. It should guide every decision that dealership employees make. Best practice is to have employees sign the code of ethics on a yearly basis to reinforce its importance.

Here is a copy of the NADA code of ethics, which can serve as a model:

> As a member of NADA, member dealers subscribe to the following principles and standards. Implicit in this Code is the requirement that NADA members comply fully with all federal, state, and local laws governing their businesses.

We pledge to:

- Operate this business in accord with the highest standards of ethical conduct.
- Treat each customer in a fair, open, and honest manner, and fully comply with all laws that prohibit discrimination.
- Meet the transportation needs of our customers in a knowledgeable and professional manner.
- Represent our products clearly and factually, standing fully behind our warranties, direct and implied, and in all other ways justifying the customer's respect and confidence.
- Advertise our products in a positive, factual, and informative manner.

- Detail charges to assist our customers in understanding repair work and provide written estimates of any service work to be performed, upon request, or as required by law.
- Resolve customer concerns promptly and courteously.
- Put our promises in writing and stand behind them.

Clear Job Descriptions

This may seem elementary, but it is not. The concept is foundational and works to both define and align operations throughout the organization.

Effective staff development is based on clear job descriptions. This approach will help avoid confusion when it comes to job responsibilities. Currently, I see that in many instances, there is no clarity over who is supposed to perform a particular function. For example, who follows up with customers who declined to purchase F&I products, the F&I department or the BDC department? Clear job descriptions eliminate any such confusion.

Schedule Regular Training

The HR manager must conduct regular training for all employees. Topics should include sales, technical product knowledge, and compliance. Training must be mandatory, documented, and required for employees to maintain employment and to get promoted.

In addition, every single employee must attend mandatory customer-satisfaction-and-retention training twice a year.

This training should be coupled with an annual review of every employee to be sure that training requirements were fulfilled.

Design Understandable Pay Plans

I mentioned this above as a function of the new all-important HR management. Let's explore it in more detail.

Nobody likes changes in pay, and dealership employees are no different. Unfortunately, it has become almost a standard operating procedure for dealer principals to change pay plans. This is demoralizing and unacceptable, and it leads to employee turnover and dissatisfaction. Employees appreciate stability, not the rollercoaster ride.

The HR director, working with senior management, needs to design and stick to clear and easy to understand pay and bonus plans for all employees.

Reduce Turnover

Every HR policy and procedure must ensure that employee turnover is reduced. That just makes good business sense. While figures vary, it is absolutely clear that hiring a new person costs money.

One national study found that the cost of replacing an employee who makes under $30,000 works out to about 16 percent of the annual salary. For someone making up to $50,000, the cost of replacement is around 50 to 60 percent of the annual salary. For executive positions, a company can expect to pay over 200 percent of the annual salary.

That's because of the many aspects involved in hiring, including the time spent interviewing, advertising costs, training, lost productivity, customers who don't like dealing with a new employee and don't return, and even changes in the corporate culture resulting from the departure of an employee. Yet most dealerships do not offer a longevity bonus to their employees.

All of these points move back to one central locus: getting it right at the beginning. HR becomes the lifeblood of the dealership—the brain that designs, implements, and maintains good policies that are long-term.

This is quite a change when it gets put in place at a dealership! I have seen it with my own eyes, when I have helped dealerships to make this important shift.

To sum up: Hiring the right person, and then training him or her, is an ongoing process; retaining the best people and promoting them is all part of the same long-term thinking and philosophy.

Though this represents a paradigm shift in the business, I believe that a healthy and strong HR department, working closely with upper management, is crucial to establishing the Perfect Dealership.

Chapter Four

Compliance

The previous chapter on human resources laid the proper foundation for the Perfect Dealership. Now let's take a look at compliance. In the following chapters, I will demonstrate how compliance applies to all departments, and I will provide some technical suggestions. In this chapter I want to highlight the importance of compliance in a Perfect Dealership. Compliance means different things to different people. Take it from me—I own a compliance company. Compliance means three things to me: a transparent sales process, improvement in employee morale, and business self-preservation.

Let's examine each in detail. First and foremost, compliance and transparency go hand in hand, and it is transparency that today's consumer is craving. It is transparency that separates on-line retailers such as Vroom from brick-and-mortar dealerships. What is the opposite of transparency? Misleading and deceptive advertising. Following state and federal advertising guidelines is the first step in the right direction. Here is another example of the opposite of transparency—payment packing and F&I product jamming. Payment packing is quoting an inflated car loan payment during a negotiation process. F&I product jamming is inserting F&I products such as service contracts and tire and wheel protection into the inflated payment without customer's consent or knowledge. Without a transparent sales process, we are only pushing customers away in search of a better sales process. And as I said before, that better option already exists, and it is digital retail. Car dealers are still in business because technology is not there 100 percent, and consumer adoption is in the beginning stages. Do not forget that consumers are willing to pay more for a better, more transparent process.

Second, improvement of employee morale is crucial. A Perfect Dealership provides a safe and clean work environment as well as ongoing training in the subjects of OSHA regulations such as emergency action planning, slip and fall prevention, ergonomics, accident prevention, and personal protective equipment. A Perfect Dealership focuses on workplace violence, workplace harassment, sexual harassment, and active shooter training. This type of training sends a clear message that the senior management team cares about its employees, and that in turn increases overall morale of the organization.

Third, it is fundamental to focus on business self-preservation. Federal and state regulators see car dealers as easy targets and low-hanging fruit. It is not uncommon to see car dealers being fined hundreds of thousands and even millions of dollars for noncompliant practices. Don't forget that federal and state investigators have political aspirations, and securing a large fine or settlement is just a stepping-stone for a future mayoral or gubernatorial race. Generating newspaper headlines is really good for their careers and really terrible for your business. Another example of business self-preservation is effective safeguarding of customer nonpublic information. Sloppy physical and computer security will translate into a data breach. Keep in mind that you have to notify all the customers affected by the data breach. If that happens, I guarantee that most of them will not come back to buy another car from your dealership. They won't even come back for an oil change!

The only way to have an effective compliance and ethics (yes, ethics) program is to appoint a compliance officer. The same way you appoint a sales manager or a service manager and hold him or her accountable for production, you need to appoint a compliance officer and hold him or her accountable for compliance training, audits, and enforcement of policies and procedures. It is absolutely critical to empower the compliance officer, and that means giving him or her authority to recommend termination of employees in all departments for violation of corporate policy. Most dealerships do not have a compliance officer! If you happen to be one of these dealers, here is what you need to do as soon as humanly possible—hire a third party to conduct compliance audits of all of the departments (sales, BDC, F&I, HR, IT, fixed ops). My company, Total Dealer Compliance, will spend the entire day in your dealership interviewing a senior management team, looking through folders, and walking through your used-car lot and service department. We will produce a final report and an action plan. This approach will help you establish a baseline. A compliance audit will reveal where your internal controls are lacking and what steps you need to take in order to improve your situation.

You also have to provide compliance training to all employees. Compliance training needs to be part of the onboarding process for new hires and ongoing training for existing employees. I recommend that you provide cloud-based compliance training, so you will have an electronic paper trail showing that your employees completed the necessary training. Total Dealer Compliance offers over 25 online courses for all employees in all departments.

Finally, I strongly suggest you take computer security seriously. Stop thinking, "This will never happen to me." Your dealership is a treasure trove of customer and employee personal information that most hackers are interested in. Your deal folders and DMS (Dealership Management System) contain names, social security numbers, driver's license numbers, dates of birth, home addresses, and employment and income information. And hackers know this! Again, you will need to hire a third party to conduct a vulnerability testing of your computer networks. They will to try break in and steal information remotely or through social engineering. They will provide a report with the list of network vulnerabilities and how to fix them. These services are not cheap, but they are totally worth it.

The real problem that we have in automotive retail is lack of professional training. There is no F&I major at a local university, and there is definitely no compliance training either. Most of us learned on the job from other people who learned on the job. This is the reason bad habits never seem to go away—that and a path of least resistance because compliance requires effort. All dealer principals, and especially absentee dealer principals, need to rely on their compliance programs and officer in order to survive in the age of transparency and proactive regulators.

Now that you have hired a compliance firm, appointed a compliance officer, and conducted vulnerability testing, you will have to rinse and repeat. Compliance is not something you do once. Compliance is an ongoing process that will slowly change your organizational culture for the better.

Don't keep your compliance program a secret. Let your customers know. Display a code of ethics on your website and in the showroom, and display compliance certificates on employees' desks. Trust me, customers will appreciate it and feel more comfortable doing business at your dealership.

Human resources and compliance are the pillars of a Perfect Dealership. Now let's examine the sales department—a true engine of a successful dealership.

Chapter Five

Sales Department

This chapter is about building the right sales team. And yet we already know two things: (1) This department will not stand on its own but will be intimately interconnected with all the other departments at your dealership, and (2) everyone will have ongoing training.

That is, interconnectedness is one key. Successful development is another: it demands a global view of the dealership, wherein ongoing training must be engaging as well as rewarding. My experience of many years in this business tells me these are the double keys to the kingdom. So, let's look at developing sales in these terms.

In summary, sales training necessitates training in (1) sales techniques, (2) product knowledge, and (3) compliance. And your sales staff must be trained as a team.

Sales Techniques

About the first: sales techniques can vary, obviously. I just want to make the point that whatever sales techniques you choose, you are setting down a process for the sales staff—a specific way to achieve the sale of a car—and this process needs to be consistent. Your staff needs to know exactly what is expected of them.

When I began in the business, I worked for a general manager who limited interactions with customers to fifteen minutes. Each salesperson got that much time on the floor to move closer to a sale by first getting the prospective buyer's personal data for a credit check. If the first person failed, a second was sent in, and, finally, the general manager would come in.

I am not necessarily advocating this method, although it worked well at the time. I'm only emphasizing that there was a clearly defined process in place, and this is crucial. We all knew what to do. You can experiment with variations on selling methods but not with the need for process to be in place to guide the staff. Just like the Big Mac that tastes the same in New York and Chicago, sales processes should be consistent regardless of which salesperson is involved. This process needs to be more of a science and less of an art. Remember that a bad process is better than no process.

Product Knowledge

This is straightforward. The salesperson should know the vehicles inside out and should be tested for this knowledge. Under no circumstances do you want the client thinking he or she knows more about the vehicle than the salesperson. Knowing everything there is to know about the car and its features will help regain some of the lost control in the sales transaction. I gave an anecdote earlier about trying to purchase a 4Runner with ventilated seats from salespeople who didn't know about the existence of said seats. Needless to say, I never went back there. Again, product knowledge among your staff must be tested. Walk-around competitions are a great way to learn the product and motivate sales staff with prizes.

Compliance Training

Not one dealership I have visited as a consultant had in-house training for compliance to state and federal laws regarding auto sales. This makes all of us an easy target for state and federal regulators, and the fines can be hefty. For example, a few years ago a Honda dealership was fined $13 million. It doesn't have to be so extreme—at the time of writing this book, a Nissan dealership in New York was fined close to $300,000. These investigations are a distraction for the dealer principal and a reputational and financial blow.

Dealerships are not large corporations with immense resources, so we tend to go to a third party for compliance training. Your state automobile dealers associations should organize these classes.

Make no mistake: compliance training is a must in a Perfect Dealership. As discussed before, dealers do not have the best reputation and often make the headlines for all the wrong reasons. My goal is to help dealers get rid of bad apples. Compliance training must be provided to all employees, especially in sales,

BDC, and F&I. They must be made aware of all federal rules and regulations that govern their jobs.

It is also a good idea for the dealer principal to hire a third party to conduct a compliance audit in a proactive move to counter potential problems and large fines. Being proactive is key when it comes to compliance. Trust me – reactive compliance is always more expensive!

At the end of the day, compliance and transparency go hand in hand, and transparency is exactly what customers are craving.

Team Building
Team building should be central to all departments, with the linkage of these teams to create a fully unified dealership as the ultimate goal.

The Perfect Dealership engages in team building also to encourage productivity and retain talent.

Traditionally, this has been a lackluster area for many employees. But culture changes over time. The most successful companies now pay attention to the value of a team mentality at work. Technology is largely about networking, after all.

One latest development is game playing as a means of building team awareness.

Team building has always been given a bad stigma as a boring activity that companies and their teams dread to take part in. Well, that has all changed thanks to the AdVenture Games (AG) team-building group. The AG team has changed how these games are played and perceived. The following article from Industry Today describes this company:

> They want to make sure that every game is not only fun and thrilling for a company, but also equips them with lifelong lessons that other team building companies do not provide you.
>
> Chad Michael, the founder of AG made it his mission to create a set of games that were not only fun to play but wanted to make sure that employees were truly learning and gaining the skills that they needed…The games teach them better communication skills, trust, how to overcome conflict and resolve problems.
>
> (From: http://industrytoday.com/article/fortune-500-companies-using-extreme-interactive-team-building-games-teach-train-employees-2017/.)

Another insight comes from Fortune.com:

> Here is the simple secret of every great place to work: It's personal—not perkonal. It's relationship-based, not transaction-based. Astoundingly, many employers still don't get that. The key to creating a great workplace…was not a prescriptive set of employee benefits, programs, and practices, but the building of high-quality relationships in the workplace.

Reaching far deeper into people than corporate benefits and cool offices ever can, those relationships are why some workers love their employers and hate to leave and why job applicants will crawl over broken glass to work at those places.

(From: http://fortune.com/2015/03/05/perfect-work place/.)

There's a lot of insight available on team building that will make you rethink it. I believe it is necessary, and it connects with my own core idea of the dealership operating as a unit across all its departments.

Management Is the Lead Team
Related to this, the management team must lead by example and participate in all training sessions and all team-building exercises. Naturally, your staff will look at this primary team as their model, and so management should be highly visible and interconnected—and available at all times versus existing in an ivory tower. The dealer principal must participate in training and demand that all employees do the same. Simply put, rank and file employees must be motivated by the behavior of the owner. This is real leadership.

Reward Your Staff
Desired behavior must be encouraged and properly rewarded. A lot of times we in the car business think that money is the ultimate reward. But, in part, times have changed, and there are numerous studies showing that there are other more effective means of motivation. Especially with the younger millennials and others, recognition is a big motivator. A simple example would be a

special parking space granted for excellence, or a reward for the employee of the month. Show appreciation in as many ways as are practical and effective.

Here is a summary of this concept that I found useful, from Forbes.

Appreciation and Access Are Also Effective

Half the companies that are both in the Fortune 500 and in the top 100 places to work did things to show their appreciation of employees. This ranged from 100,000 hours of free massages at Google, to the vice-chair at NetApp calling 10–20 employees a day who had gotten caught "doing something right," to internal tech conferences at Qualcomm, to safety bonuses, personalized notes, special luncheons, actively recognizing and supporting diversity, low-cost health insurance for part-time employees and health and wellness centers. Whatever form it took, employees at these companies felt appreciated by their leadership.

(From: http://www.forbes.com/sites/georgebradt/ 2014/03/12/how-the-best-fortune-500-companies-to-work-for-drive-appreciation-access-rewards-2/#541a4a7865de.)

Another point made here was to give employees access—access to top management and even some decision-making. Whole Foods is good at this and organizes field trips to give staff a chance to voice opinions and sometimes even help get policy implemented.

Smaller businesses can do more of all of these things: show appreciation to staff, reward them, and also give them access. Car dealerships, being smaller, actually have an edge here.

A Final Word on Training in This Chapter
There must be a curriculum of courses that every employee has to take in order to accomplish a corporate level of training. New hires (sales, BDC, F&I, parts, service, receptionists) cannot be allowed customer-facing interactions unless they complete mandatory training.

Let me add that receptionist training is especially important because this is the first person who interacts with the customer, and there is no room for error.

The Internet as the New Sales Platform
The Internet is here to stay, and it may well dominate every aspect of our lives. The car business is not immune to this development. Dealers need to embrace the Internet and e-commerce and use it to their advantage.

First and foremost, your dealer website must be easy to use and full of useful information that allows the customer to research as much as possible.

Your dealer website must work on all devices and provide necessary functionality on the go. Customers should be able to schedule a test drive, book a service appointment, and purchase parts and accessories online. In other words, they must be able to move in the direction of a purchase or service appointment, and do as much as possible of these online.

The dealer website must be transactional, and yes, that means that at some point in the very near future, customers will be able to buy a car from the comfort of their home. I see that most dealers are afraid to embrace this future because they fear loss of profit that might come with the total transparency that Internet commerce brings. There is no need to fight the future. Forget about it. Embrace it instead. Digital retail is here to stay! Would you rather make a little less for a long period of time or make as much as you can now and be gone in a few years?

I strongly believe that whoever masters online transactional car sales will dominate the market. Also, selling cars online will open up new markets to enterprising dealers. And that means that dealers need to start thinking about logistics—shipping cars and parts across the country.

Currently most consumers buy cars from local dealers; however, providing a transparent, online, Amazon-type experience will allow dealers to reach customers in other geographical areas.

There are several transactional sales platforms in development, and dealers need to start evaluating them ASAP and choose the one that they like the most. It is mission critical for the Perfect Dealership to get into the online sales game early.

There are companies out there that have raised tremendous capital (some were mentioned in the preface) and are getting into online sales of used cars. They are Vroom, Shift, Carvanna, and Roadster. Dealers need to recognize that consumers are responding positively to no-haggle pricing, home deliveries, and a "no questions asked" return policy. Dealers must adapt to these new market conditions. Similar to buying from Amazon and enjoying the convenience it provides, once customers start buying used cars online, they will expect a similar experience when shopping for a new car. The Perfect Dealership better be there providing an amazing digital retail experience.

Perfect Dealership Utilizes Videos on Its Website

I recommend how-to videos. Examples: how to use a GPS, how to change the oil yourself (again, appeal to the DIY community), and how to remove a hard top. This approach makes the dealer's website a destination worth visiting instead of having customers go to YouTube and view competitors' videos.

Software—CRM, Dealertrack, VAuto, and So Forth

Software is becoming crucial in day-to-day operations, and dealers need to evaluate what software better suits their needs. Price alone should never be the determining factor.

Once the dealer determines what software to use, then actually using all of its capabilities becomes paramount. The best CRM (Customer Relationship Management) is not going to improve operations if not used properly. Make sure that vendors provide unlimited training on how to use the software. You are paying good money every month for this product, so demand solid training.

Provide Tools for Consumers to Simplify the Buying Process

Soft pull/preapproval and trade-appraisal tools that provide hard numbers must be utilized.

Software in general has to simplify the sales and service process as well as the customer's experience. For example, if you are using software to schedule service appointments, then you should make sure that the service advisor is ready when the customer drops off the car. Another example: when the customer schedules a test drive, the car needs to be ready to go when the customer comes to the dealership. The bottom line is this: software is important, but what gets the job done is the human interaction it enables.

Schedule: Quality of Life Is Important—Stop Having People Work Bell to Bell

We addressed this in the HR section, but it is worth repeating. There has to be a balance, and it is unacceptable to have bell-to-bell schedules. This is one of the primary reasons for turnover. Working long hours contributes to burnout and, paradoxically, reduced productivity. Favor brains over brute force or burnout—your own brain, that is, working to promote productivity among your staff in ways you probably have not tried before.

Employee Pricing

One of the employee benefits should be an employee pricing. This employee pricing should extend to cars, parts, labor, and accessories. Employee pricing should extend to the employee's family members. Trust me, your employees will appreciate it!

Marketing and Public Relations

If you are still advertising in your local newspaper, you are throwing your money away.

The Perfect Dealership dominates online marketing. This starts with the responsive, transactional website described above. Google advertising is key, since almost every single customer goes online before stepping foot in a car dealership.

I know that some of you out there are not huge fans of Cars. com, Autotrader.com, and so forth, but these websites are an integral part of consumers' shopping processes, and the Perfect Dealership needs to have a presence on all of these websites. I never understood dealers who prefer one over the other. The Perfect Dealership has a presence on Cars.com, Autotrader.com, Cargurus.com, and so forth. Presence and frequency are the two pillars of advertising.

E-mail marketing is another key, a way to keep customers engaged and help them transition from sales to service and back to sales. Another effective approach to stay in touch with customers is through the text messaging and push notifications since customers pay less and less attention to e-mails.

Most dealers spend a vast majority of advertising dollars on attracting new customers. My advice is to allocate a portion of the advertising budget to service marketing and data mining. It is mission critical to retain the customer after the sale and make sure that customers are coming back to perform scheduled maintenance and repairs. If we treat our customers well in the service department, they will buy another car from our sales department.

Unfortunately dealers across the country do not have the best reputation, and there is very little effort by brick-and-mortar dealers to change this. The Perfect Dealership retains a public relations firm to promote its message throughout the community and broader markets. It is a good idea to be engaged with local high schools and colleges in order to promote careers in automotive retail. Through leadership articles in local publications, showcase the fact that the dealership is a responsible corporate citizen.

Loyalty Program

Also, create a reward/loyalty program for every dollar that the customer spends in the dealership. Here is a good explanation of why there is a need for rewards programs:

> What exactly is a loyalty program, then? While the specifics of each program may differ, the premise remains the same: a loyalty program is a marketing system instituted by a business that rewards purchasing behavior, thus increasing the customers' urge to stay loyal to the company. A loyalty program may offer convenience, store credit, prizes, or any other benefit that would entice the loyalty of a customer.
>
> (http://marketingland.com/8-reasons-loyalty-pro-grams-imperative-marketers-109077.)

Our customers are familiar with and use loyalty programs every day when they go to Starbucks, Walgreens, and Exxon Mobil gas stations. Again, implementing the loyalty program is the key, and that means regular training of salespeople, finance managers, BDC, service writers, and parts countermen. But trust me—it is not as easy as it sounds.

Reputation Management

We live in the age of reviews, and customers pay attention. The Perfect Dealership encourages its customers to leave reviews on all available platforms (Google, Yelp, DealerRater, and the dealer's website). You can't just hope that reviews will miracu-lously appear; a process needs to be followed after every de-livery. It is a good idea to send an e-mail to customers with links to Google, Yelp, and so forth. Another approach is to utilize a software solution that populates the review on all platforms. You can also incentivize customers through discounts on future visits to the service department and incentivize salespeople by instituting a bonus for the most reviews collected. Another crucial element is that negative reviews need to be addressed immediately. In a Perfect Dealership, the compliance officer, general manager and dealer principal are actively engaged in resolving negative reviews; these reviews cannot be left unanswered. Unanswered negative reviews are a sign of a business that doesn't care about its customers and its own reputation. Oftentimes leaving a negative review is a last resort, and that means that the dealership failed at basic complaint resolution. It is a good idea to have a "File a Complaint" tab on the dealership's website. This complaint must be immediately routed to the compliance officer, general manager and dealer principal for timely resolution. Trust me, you can turn customer complaints into glowing Internet reviews!

Home Delivery
I know that most old-school car guys want to get the customer into the showroom, but the business landscape is changing. Companies such as Vroom, Shift, and most leasing companies pride themselves on simplifying the buying process and providing home/office delivery. Again, the Perfect Dealership adapts to the new market conditions and perfects the process.

Perfect Dealerships need to start thinking about developing delivery/logistics departments, especially once digital retail becomes a reality. Dealers have to start figuring out staffing for local and interstate deliveries.

Be Active in the Community

Dealers still generate most of their sales from their local markets. Therefore, dealers must be active in the local community. This can be accomplished by sponsoring local youth teams, offering summer internships to college and high school students, and fundraising for local needs. Social responsibility is a priority for a Perfect Dealership. This is related to loyalty, which is a two-way street. Never forget that your proximity to your community gives you an immense advantage to earn their loyalty. If you don't, you didn't try hard enough.

Mastering the Internet to Expand Your Geographical Range

Setting the obvious advantage of a local market aside for a moment, transactional online sales will expand the dealer's market, as I mentioned before. It will not be uncommon to sell cars to people one hundred or one thousand miles away. The sooner the dealer gets into this business, the better. There is an opportunity now to master interstate shipping, logistics, and online marketing by selling parts online. It is possible to have a fully functioning e-commerce website in your parts department. If you can master selling parts online, then selling cars will be a walk in the park.

Product-Knowledge Specialist to Deliver the Car

Given that cars become more and more technologically advanced, it is really important that you deliver via an expert who can explain how to use all the gadgets. Apple's Genius Bar is a good model. Customers should be able to get in touch with a product specialist to answer their questions. BMW is already moving in this direction. One solution is to have a delivery team composed of people who know each car inside out. Keep in mind that customers have a hard time digesting all the information at the time of delivery, so the dealer needs a process where customers can come back for the second delivery or a new-car clinic. Another solution is to create a video explaining all the gadgets and how to use them and post the video on the dealership's website. I have yet to see this proactive approach in most dealerships. The more we help our customers, the higher our chances of retaining them.

In essence I'm saying this: We were once a business that got away with subpar customer service. People became used to this, but now it is the customer who is in control. Surprise them with your adaptation to the new conditions by being there at every step for them. Have a website that is immensely informative, transparent, and enabling; a staff that is admirably trained and a joy to deal with; and interconnected departments that help one another pursue the common goal of helping the customer. Give like a dedicated professional, and you'll receive.

You will then make a good living. No one will be able to take it away from you, not even Amazon, because you are on the ground in your own community and have the edge, representing excellence and showing civic responsibility where everyone knows your name, face, and reputation.

Chapter Six

BDC Department

Importance of the BDC

There were times when dealers didn't have BDC departments. Times have changed, and it is now impossible to run a successful dealership without an efficient BDC department. In other words, this is no longer optional, but through its own contributions and efficiency, a good BDC should more than pay for itself. Do not get trapped in the old model in an attempt to resist change or be frugal. Effective customer communication is key, and a BDC department is the answer.

Hence, Perfect Dealerships will continue investing in BDC departments and their infrastructure. That means better software, higher payroll, faster computers, and more authority to conduct a deal from A to Z. The importance of your BDC department will continue to grow, and dealers will have to come to terms with the fact that a qualified BDC manager will be earning on par with a sales manager. Effectively, the central command of a dealership has expanded to add an arm. As discussed in the HR chapter, a BDC manager must be have the necessary training and authority to execute relevant policy and procedures.

Function

The BDC answers e-mails, takes calls, makes appointments and makes outgoing follow-up calls. As such, it is the noncustomer-facing voice of the dealership. Good customer relations and service are achieved here as well, no longer just on the sales floor or in the service department. This situation has come into being because so much of our world now is virtual, cell-phone mediated, or moving that way; hence, the BDC integrates with the new environment wherein the customer now rules.

The Customer Is Now in Control

This is an essential point, as important as the handful of other key concepts in this book, such as ongoing training. The dealer who believes he or she is still in control, with something of a captive market for a product everyone needs is living in a time capsule. The necessity of the BDC is related to this reversal of control. The more capable, well-informed, and appropriately demanding the client (who now has more good choices than ever before), the better the organization needed to meet and to accommodate this new breed of client, at every step.

Quick Response

Keep this principle in mind. The new environment we live in, especially with the new and ever-expanding influence of technology, will necessarily help to define the Perfect Dealership.

Quickness of response is another recent exigency. It was always relevant, but now it cannot be neglected and will separate winners from losers. We live in the on-demand age and need access to information at all hours of the day. Car dealerships need to realize that and provide transparent information at all times. And I don't mean an auto-responder e-mail.

One way to satisfy this 24-7 demand by the controlling customer—who wants information or wants to make steps toward a sale—is to design what is now being called a hybrid BDC. This is where you outsource a part of the operation. For example, functions can be handled in-house from 9:00 a.m. to 9:00 p.m., and the remaining twelve-hour slot can be handled by outsourcing, so that chat is always available, and any questions can be intelligently answered. Second-generation chat providers are worth looking into. Beware of doing this on the cheap with third-world operations. We all know the difference (although there are possibly a few exceptional outfits out there). Amex and Discover do not outsource to inferior operations, for example, and they are leaders.

In addition, put all the relevant data on your website. Data such as pricing, interest rates, F&I products, product review, and so forth. Days of not fully disclosing the price are in the past. Whenever I see "Too Low to Show" on the dealers website or "Call for Price" I know that this particular dealership still thinks that it is 1985.

Nothing is more disconcerting than getting a reply late at night that feels unrehearsed, by a foreign company or other company that is not trained and is going through the motions only to make some money, and so the customer is not getting anywhere. You may well lose this customer right at this juncture.

In other words, if you are going to have a BDC, do it right! Be available through all possible channels (telephone, e-mail, chat, text, and video), and this availability will contribute to additional sales. People are willing to pay a premium for good service.

I remember losing my wallet once on a Sunday night. The *only* bank among several to help me with my lost card was Charles Schwab. They FedExed a new card to me, and I had it the next day. The call was taken by an educated English speaker who could relate to me exactly. This bank is a class act, and I have retained my relationship to Charles Schwab to this day.

Customer Relations Management Software

CRM (customer relations management) is the brain of your operation. The software is expensive and can cost you around $1,500 per month. Still, most dealerships I have consulted for do not use all the functionality available in these CRMs. This is very much their loss and a waste of their own money. Make sure that employees are fluent in using the CRM. Most CRM providers have trainers that come out to the dealership as well as online training for every subject. In the Perfect Dealership, CRM training is ongoing and mandatory.

We operate inside a very limited universe, so it is possible to anticipate just about everything: the questions that arise, the answers needed, every service or protocol, and the sequences. The CRM is a limited but important artificial intelligence that should become your best friend. Get to know it, and by all means, use all of its assets.

Staying in Touch with the Customer for a Lifetime
Many dealers make the mistake of devoting most of their energy to selling cars and allocating very little effort to retaining the customer. The cost of acquisition of a new customer is significantly higher than retaining an existing one.

Here is a valuable quotation that encompasses most of the relevant points:

> The lifetime value of a customer includes everything they will ever buy from you today, tomorrow, and in the years ahead—and the cost of acquiring a new customer is estimated to be 20 times greater than keeping an existing customer happy.
>
> (https://www.linkedin.com/pulse/what-cost-customer-acquisition-vs-retention-ian-kingwill.)

Hence, the BDC department needs to dedicate a large portion of its efforts toward retaining sold customers. Long-term thinking is a major shift in your philosophy that gets real results. This is a very different kind of mentality, and the perspicacious dealer principal will be very much aware of this transition as it occurs. What I mean is that you will be fascinated to watch this transformation take hold of your own operations as you shift toward long-term strategies. There is nothing like it! It is a truly transformative moment in your career to begin see things long term like this and to act accordingly. This starts when retention of the customer becomes your ultimate goal, versus a shorter-term mentality that almost excludes real relationships.

That means transitioning these customers to all departments: sales, service, parts, body shop, and back to sales. The BDC manager needs to work closely with the general manager and the parts-and-service director to make sure that the dealership is in touch with each and every customer. In this way, BDC becomes another centralizing hub in the dealership to help with this essential interconnectedness, but it now includes your ongoing clients.

And that means allocating more dollars to the BDC budget.

Do not think that paying a minimum wage will produce high-quality, efficient BDC employees, and do not think that $50,000 a year will get you a qualified BDC manager.

Online Transactions
As more sales will take place online, the BDC department must develop a new function of online sales support and be available to the customer through every step of the sale. This is a wonderful, achievable goal. Related to this is letting the customer complete as much of the sale online as is possible—if not all of it!—first through information that encourages and directs self-education. Armed with this knowledge, the customer then makes the specific choices for the vehicle he or she will purchase. (Amazon is selling Fiats online in Italy now. This is their first move forward into our market, and the sales are all being done online!)

Coordination of BDC with the Delivery Department
The BDC department must coordinate with the delivery department in order to have a smooth home/office delivery process. This is the crowning moment of the sale—when the customer receives the car from you. You have won them over against all the competition out there and completed the deal. The utmost care

and appreciation must be apparent in your delivery of the car that you have done your very best to provide them with—like a father delivering the bride (just kidding, but…you should be almost that careful).

Remember that buying a car is the second-largest purchase our customers make. Let's make it memorable!

The One-Price Model

In the car business we either love the one-price model or we hate it. I am not going to argue for one approach or the other, but I strongly feel that Amazon and Uber are changing the buying habits of consumers everywhere. We are getting used to being able to buy pretty much everything online and then have it delivered to our house or workplace. At some point in the not so distant future, consumers will demand the same experience when buying a car. Dealers need to anticipate this and be prepared. The only way online transactions can take place is via the one-price model. The one-price model will also improve customer satisfaction, as the sales process is completely transparent. Consumers will pay more for a transparent, no-surprise experience. I live in New York City and oftentimes use Uber, which in some instances is more expensive than yellow cabs, but I am willing to pay for transparency and convenience. Car sales are no different.

BDC Training and Compliance Training

The Perfect Dealership has ongoing training, and BDC training is a huge part of it. No one escapes this exigency. And that training should feel rewarding and compel the trainees to perfect their skills in a way that motivates them and gives them self-respect. The better you are at your work, the more proud of it you should feel!

Skill-based training as well as compliance training must now be mandatory. Your BDC staff needs to know how to use the CRM software or any other software inside out. They should have access to DMS and know how to structure a deal. They must develop excellent communication skills and perfect organizational skills in order to provide effective follow-up. In the successful follow-up lies part of the secret to retaining your customers, which is long-term thinking, which in turn is stability, and stability is success.

Compliance training must focus on the Do Not Call and CAN-SPAM Acts, safeguards rule, red flags rule, disposal rule, and privacy rule. BDC staff needs to know how to safeguard and dispose of customer's nonpublic information, know when it is OK to contact the customer, and craft e-mails that are not deceptive. Again, compliance training contributes to transparency and improves the overall sales process.

Second-Generation Chat Platforms

Dealers need to transition to second-generation chat platforms for both sales and service. These chat platforms are available 24-7. You will be able to see what pages the customer is visiting before initiating contact. More importantly, a Perfect Dealership is open twenty-four hours, and having second-generation chat platforms on your digital storefront is not a bad idea, especially because so many customers are doing research late at night from the comfort of their living rooms. We need to be there at all hours of the day. We can't just ask the consumer to fill out a form and let them know that someone will reach out to them in the morning.

Chat platforms will fail unless you have dedicated chat staff and there is a process in place for chat follow-up.

Remember that 30 percent of all chats are fixed-ops related, so it is a good idea to have a chat line for service customers, especially for the Do-It-Yourself (DIY) community. For example, Microcenter computer stores cater heavily to the Build-It-Yourself community and has been a leader in PC sales nationwide—bring in the enthusiasts.

Conclusion
BDC has arrived due to technology and heightened competition. We live in a 24-7 world now, and the dealership will be interacting with clients around the clock or will itself have to go to sleep forever and take the proverbial "dirt nap." BDC is effectively customer service that has been extended to deal with the new conditions of the auto industry. Ultimately Perfect Dealerships attract real talent to their BDC departments and allocate more and more funds to improve operations. Every day and every year, BDC departments are becoming more and more important to the survival in the digital age.

Chapter Seven

Service and Parts Department

Again, all departments must work toward a common goal. That common goal is defined by the organization's mission statement. Great companies such as Hewlett Packard took this statement seriously, placing it at the very core of their values and mode of operating. They and others like them proved that when you have a worthy ideal *and actually implement it*, great things can happen.

A lot of times I see that there is a total disconnect between the service and sales departments. An effective BDC is one attempt to connect all these departments that usually develop the normal headaches with one another or even rivalries and animosities. But we should not rely wholly on a BDC for connectivity and integration. Don't use halfway solutions for a problem; don't put lipstick on a pig.

For example, there can be animosity because the sales department feels it is being overcharged for the used-car prep. I am a strong believer in the sales department paying the customer-pay labor rate for used-car prep work. It doesn't mean that service department has a license to charge whatever it wants. Service managers must understand that high repair orders only make used cars less competitive and harder to sell. The longer it takes the sales department to turn the inventory, the less used cars there will be to prep. This understanding demonstrates respect for the work and also a sense of fairness—which is how to get people to want to work together toward shared goals.

There should be regular meetings between the general sales manager and the service manager to coordinate transition of customers from sales to service and back to sales. In other words, never let go of the customer. It is in everybody's interest to ensure customer retention.

A few more suggestions follow.

Service Department Introduction
The sales department absolutely must introduce every customer to the service department. And I am not talking about a nominal thirty second walk around. This must be an active introduction during the dealership walk-around—to make the customer feel comfortable and know where to go when the first oil change is due. It is a good idea to introduce service advisors and the service manager. In the age of digital retail, the Perfect Dealership must provide a virtual dealership walk-around that showcases the service and parts departments. Customers need to see the latest equipment, OEM parts, and technicians' certificates.

New-Car Clinics
Schedule new-car clinics on a regular basis. As cars become more complicated, customers need help figuring out how to use all the gadgets. It is unrealistic to expect customers to understand how to interface their cell phone and use GPS, satellite radio, and other apps during the delivery process. There is also a need for an encore delivery (secondary delivery a week later), and new-car clinics can solve the problem.

These new-car clinics need to be promoted in the showroom and the dealer's website and take place on a regular basis, monthly or quarterly. They should take place at night so customers can visit after work. Snacks and soft drinks should be provided. Technicians should teach customers how to use basic controls and answer questions. Again, these clinics serve a dual purpose: helping customers learn how to use their new car and also gain familiarity and feel comfortable with the service department.

Fix Cars Right the First Time
This is the heart and soul of a successful service department. Regular technician training must be mandatory and quality control must be made a priority. It is essential to have A techs oversee the work of B and C techs.

It is also a good idea to display your technicians' certificates and relevant information in the customer waiting area, so customers know that factory-trained technicians using OEM parts are working on their cars. Factory training and OEM parts are the reasons to use the service department instead of an independent mechanic. Furthermore, OEM parts and OEM-trained mechanics are the only reasons to charge higher prices compared to independents.

Competitive Pricing

Service departments have an uphill battle when it comes to bringing the customers back. Service retention gets lower and lower with every visit to the department. One of the reasons is the perception that this service is expensive. This issue needs to be addressed head-on. One approach is to actively shop competition (both franchise dealers and independent mechanics). Especially, look at competitive work such as oil changes and brake jobs. Make sure that your prices are in line with the competition. It is a good idea to have a board displaying local competitors' prices. Do for the customers first what they will do on their cell phones anyway for cost research. Convey transparency in all your operations, hopefully ahead of Amazon and others that will soon be doing so.

The Service Department Is in the Sales Business

Every time I visit a service department, I have a feeling that service advisors are the opposite of the salespeople. You cannot assume you will make a sale, but it seems to be the mind-set with many service writers that cars inevitably break—so they have a passive strategy. Another problem that contributes to the lack of sales in service departments is understaffing. I am a big believer that an effective service advisor needs to spend time with each customer in order to get to know him or her and the car and upsell the necessary work, and in order to do that, the service advisor needs to see no more than twelve to fifteen customers per day. If your service advisors are seeing more than fifteen customers per day, what you have is order takers. And order takers do not make money!

Service managers must have regular sales meetings to outline their goals and methods for accomplishing them. Also, sales training and phone-skills training must be mandatory for service advisors. The strategy of sitting back and waiting for the calls and being rather vague about pricing the repairs is a pathetic modus operandi. Every way of generating money at a dealership requires care and training. Every problem offers an opportunity to learn and be better at finding solutions and generating profit next time. Management has to care and demonstrate exemplary attention, and this attitude has to permeate the whole staff.

As an aside, the police academy in my neighborhood was recently training the new cadets. One morning, I was out by 6:00 a.m., and I saw the instructors arrive at John Jay College. Their shirts were perfectly pressed, they carried heavy duffel bags, and their belts were loaded up with devices and a big summons book. What struck me was their perfection of appearance and their matching attitudes. The three of them said nothing as they walked past me, but they projected seriousness and meticulous attention to detail. Alert and focused, they personified their leadership position. There could be no doubt they were instructors.

Later that day when I returned, the cadets were exiting the same classroom building. Their appearances mimicked that of their instructors, down to every last detail. Their young, inexperienced faces lacked the same intensity of focus, but the influence was obvious. I could see that their leaders were passing along the right discipline.

The message is, of course, excellent leadership. There are truly not enough examples around us in everyday life. When something seems to work this well, I think we should all study it and learn from it and take the parts that apply to our own discipline. The right role model at the top can influence countless others below him or her.

Service Advisor Walk-Around
For most drivers, going to a car dealership's service drive is the equivalent of going to a dental appointment—with one major difference. During both, the customer sits in the waiting room, flips through magazines, and hopes for the best when his or her name is called. But what makes these two scenarios different is that when it comes to their dental work, most people go to the same dentist for several years, maybe even decades. For dealership visits, that's not always the case. Customers will often take their cars to many different locations over time to maintain their cars.

That's why it is critical to make a positive first impression and build a long-lasting relationship with every customer. One specific way to do so is to conduct a walk-around when the customer comes in for schedule maintenance or repairs. During an active walk-around, a service writer inspects the car with the owner, which can dramatically increase the chances of up-selling additional maintenance or repair work. Together, the customer and the service advisor will inspect the most common areas—body of the car, tire pressure, mileage, and service history—to get to know the car better. Inspecting the body of the car and asking questions such as, "Hey, I noticed these scratches; do you want me to get you an estimate?" help generate additional body work.

An active walk-around is essential when you consider that parts and service is extremely profitable business for dealerships. In fact, car dealerships yield much higher margins selling labor and parts than they do selling cars. No matter where you are in the United States, the profit margin on labor is about 75 percent and on parts it is between 40 and 50 percent. A Perfect Dealership trains its service advisors to perform an active walk-around at all times, so it becomes a natural part of their daily routine. This will (pardon the pun) "drive" customer satisfaction and retention, repurchase rates, and overall revenue.

Just like seeing the same dentist can help a patient cultivate a relationship that inspires confidence and trust—let alone deal more easily with the pain of any procedure—dealers should make every effort to inspire their customers to visit their service department whenever a need arises. This approach will build the relationship between the dealer, the customer, and the car.

Multipoint Vehicle Inspection

Multipoint vehicle inspection (MVPI) must be utilized on every single car, and maintenance/repair recommendations must be made based on this MPVI.

Menu selling should be utilized with every customer, similar to what we do in the F&I department. This approach ensures 100 percent presentation of proposed maintenance and repairs to 100 percent of customers, 100 percent of the time.

Service advisors need to utilize software and all channels of communication to communicate with customers and get authorization to do the work. That means using e-mail and text messages, not just leaving voice mail. There are plenty of good software solutions that explain in a professional manner why the customer needs to perform certain maintenance/repair work. This is especially true with leased cars, which need to be returned in good shape. This professional proposal is sent via e-mail. Customers should be able to decline or approve the work right from the e-mail.

Declined work must be followed up on a regular basis. Persistence is a virtue. Be authoritative, and offer excellent information as a way of retaining customer interest. Anything less and your effort could be perceived as an annoying sales call.

BDC in the Service Department
Again, BDC is an attempt to centralize operations. The department should have an overview of each customer's experiences and needs at the dealership. It should constantly track these experiences and follow up on matters. As such, BDC will interface with all other departments.

Service managers need to work closely with the BDC department to improve customer experience. This is the stated goal, the mission. Stay focused on this one thing—put it ahead of your own personal or departmental agenda—and you will all work better together. Then you will be a team. It will require leadership to instill these noncompetitive patterns in your staff. One idea is this: have a monthly recognition prize for the best cooperation between two staff members that resulted in two departments or more generating better service together, hold this in the highest esteem, and award it at a meeting of all staff.

Appointments
The BDC should handle appointments. It must make convenient appointments for customers and not bring everybody in at 7:30 a.m. and hope for the best—a sure way to alienate customers.

BDC staff must find out if the customer will be waiting for the car or whether they will need a loaner or a rental.

Most people work during the day, and it is hard to get to a service department. I think that more service departments should be open till midnight and repair cars through the night. The service department in a perfect dealership recognizes that convenience matters to customers and accommodates them in every way possible.

Appointment setting must work in conjunction with shop-loading software to result in (a) the least amount of wait time and (b) the most qualified tech performing the work.

Effective Communication

Effective communication is a strength that a lot of service departments sorely lack. A lot of times the service writer can't be reached on the phone, or once he or she is on the phone, the customer can't get a straight answer.

A friend of mine told me he called Mercedes Manhattan the other day. He has a beloved E Series model that needs a new key and possibly a new ignition switch and steering lock. These parts all involve security, in order to start the car. The dealership needs to program—this is its leverage—and the work can be expensive. The woman answering tried to deflect her complete lack of knowledge of this car's electronic ignition system by stating over and over that she could not be specific, and she became hostile as my friend pressed for more information. The essence of his customer experience was hostility arising from ignorance. This is exactly what we want to avoid. The more knowledgeable and trained the service writer, the less likely he or she will fly off the handle or simply botch the call to cover up for his or her own ignorance.

Service Price Guide

Independent shops are usually much better when it comes to phone skills and making appointments. People doing the phone work will often be in close proximity to the techs and will learn about all kinds of repairs and their related issues, day after day. Service managers should mystery-shop their staff as well as their competition to perfect the process.

For most customers, service is about cost. The customer is calling to find out what the cost of the repair is going to be, as in the Mercedes story above. Again, many service advisors fail to provide a definitive answer. A good strategy to combat this issue is to utilize a price guide in the DMS system. The service manager should set the prices for the most commonly requested work, and service advisors can pull up the information on the fly.

Using a service price guide is essential; it allows service advisors to provide accurate, quick, and consistent price quotes for labor. Quick and accurate quotes increase customer satisfaction and profit. Dealer-management software such as Reynolds & Reynolds, ADP, and Dealertrack have developed sophisticated service price guides that are easy to use and increase productivity.

Unfortunately many dealers are not using this valuable tool. As a result, customers receive information that is inaccurate, or it just takes too long for the service advisor to track down the price of parts and labor. We live in a fast-paced world, and service customers expect a quick and accurate quote as opposed to being put on hold for an indefinite amount of time.

Whenever I mystery-shop service departments, all too often I encounter service advisors who can't provide a job quote in a timely manner or the price is too high, and that's the best-case scenario. In a worst-case scenario I am put on "permahold" or transferred to someone's voice mail. In comparison, when I mystery-shop independents, they are generally better at providing quotes more quickly, and their quotes are usually lower compared to franchised dealers.

Answering a customer's inquiry is the first and only opportunity for the service department to impress and convince the customer to do business. Use of a service price guide conveys a sense of professionalism and contributes to the bottom line. There is also a correlation between quick and accurate quotes and an increased appointment ratio. Moreover, service advisors can easily convert a saved quote into an appointment at a later point in time. To maximize profitability, service price guides have additional modules that provide recommendations for related repairs and scheduled maintenance. Communicating these recommendations will ensure repeat business and additional revenue.

In a Perfect Dealership, the service manager configures the service price guide and runs a utilization report on a daily basis to ensure that service advisors are using it. Again, implementation and utilization of service price guide will increase profit and customer satisfaction.

Wear a Uniform
The Perfect Dealership transmits professionalism at every level. We need to make sure that service advisors, porters, and even

cashiers wear a uniform. First, a uniform identifies employees and showcases professionalism that many dealerships lack. It goes without saying that uniforms must be clean, and name tags should be worn by all employees.

Training

To repeat yet again the key concept of this book, the Perfect Dealership trains its staff on a regular basis. Service technicians must be up to date with factory training. Service writers need sales training and phone-skills training. And every employee in the service department needs customer-service training. Think of what a good surgeon, teacher, or athlete goes through—always learning, always trying to improve—and don't devalue your own work, whatever it is. "All things excellent are as difficult as they are rare," a great man wrote.

Retention

Customers' satisfaction in the service department is mission critical to customer retention and purchasing the next car from the same dealership. In fact, to put it the other way around, it should almost guarantee an ongoing relationship with a customer if you fix their car right the first time at a reasonable cost and perhaps even repeat this process. Then, you likely have a loyal client.

To better transition the customer back to sales from service, it is important to utilize data-mining software to determine if there is equity in their car. There should be a well-defined process between the service department and sales to make the transition smooth and profitable.

It is a good idea to have a dedicated sales department with salespeople, a sales manager, and a finance manager housed right in the service department. In many cases, customers can get into the new car for less than the cost of the repair order and still keep the payment the same. As of the writing of this book, prices have gotten very competitive for new purchases and leases; and this fact—how reasonable is the cost for a new car versus repairing an older car—can ensure a sale or lease. (When I ran dealerships, we made this happen all the time. The numbers were often compelling and made the sale happen.)

So, synergy between sales and service is essential. Similar to the sales department, the service department must motivate its service advisors and technicians to generate sales. There should be a bonus plan to motivate staff to go the extra mile. Don't let these incentives destroy teamwork and synergy, however. This comes down to leadership and perhaps shared incentives, when sales and service cooperate well.

Safety/OSHA/Cleanliness
The Perfect Dealership provides clean and safe facilities. OSHA regulation must be followed, and related training must be provided to all employees on a regular basis. The service department must be prepared for an OSHA inspector visit at all times. OSHA fines are really high and can have a devastating impact on the bottom line. Keep in mind that OSHA raised its fines in 2016; however, through good management, all of these fines can be avoided. Compliance training must be a part of regular training. It all starts with the cleanliness of the shop floor; this is the first thing that an OSHA inspector will look at. If there are oil and antifreeze spills on the floor, that means you do not have an effective slip-and-fall-prevention program. And this factor alone will make the OSHA inspector look further. Looking further means checking if the electrical circuits are overloaded, fire exits are blocked,

eyewash station is operational, and so forth. I did consulting for a dealer in South Carolina, and his service department was absolutely spotless. I asked the service manager how he did it, and he said something that I will never forget: "If you got time to lean, you got time to clean."

Marketing and Merchandising

Service departments make money by selling parts and labor. There is an additional way to generate extra income through effective merchandising, but very little attention is paid to maximizing sales in the retail shop. In a Perfect Dealership, service managers focus on four metrics to measure the success of the retail shop: customer traffic, conversion rate, number of items per purchase, and sales profits before costs. There are simple steps that can be taken to address this problem:

- offer accessories and impulse buy items
- have prices on all items
- display "Was and Now" sale prices
- promote the retail shop via your website and marketing efforts
- offer products for the DIY community

Marketing is essential for a successful service department. What I usually see is that almost every advertising dollar is spent on new car sales. We need to change that. In the Perfect Dealership, the dealer principal and the senior management team understand that it is mission critical to advertise their service and parts departments. The service business is as important as sales and much more profitable. It is not uncommon to see a 75 percent markup on labor and 45 percent markup on parts.

The service manager has to design an effective marketing campaign that utilizes all the channels. The Perfect Dealership's service department promotes itself on the dealership's website, through OEM mailers, Google AdWords, and so forth. Speaking of Google AdWords, I encourage you to Google "oil change" and your zip code. You will be surprised that it is mainly independent shops that dominate this page.

Another important aspect of effective marketing is to attract customers who are out of factory warranty. Service retention is really low for out-of-warranty customers; however, this is the most profitable repair work that a dealership can perform. There needs to be an active outreach to bring these customers back.

Selling Parts Online
Another source of revenue for the parts and service department is to sell parts online. Similar to selling cars online, dealers can enter distant markets through online sales. The best approach is to put the entire parts catalogue online with pictures, full descriptions, and an integrated shopping cart. It is also important to promote online parts sales through all channels. There are software solutions that simplify this selling of parts online. If the dealership is not selling parts online, they are making it so much easier for parts stores and Amazon to dominate the market.

Cater to the Do-It-Yourself Community
Dealers need to cater to the DIY community by offering prepackaged oil change kits and other similar products through their online shop and in the retail shop. We need to bring back these customers to the dealership from aftermarket parts stores.

Quick Lube

Perfect Dealerships offer quick lube service without an appointment, in order to compete with independents. Over the last couple of decades most OEMs realized that they were losing service customers to independent providers such as Jiffy Lube and Valvoline. According to NADA, car dealers are only capturing 23 percent of the oil-change market. That realization triggered a worldwide rollout of dealer-branded quick lube/express service operations. Unfortunately, many dealers are not maximizing sales opportunities in their quick lube/express service operations.

Customers were not coming back to the dealership for their immediate maintenance needs due to inconvenience, perceived high price, and ineffective phone skills of dealership employees. OEM quick lube/express service is designed to address all these issues. In order for the dealership to increase its market share of oil changes, it needs to create awareness. First, the dealer's website has to have a page dedicated to quick lube. Second, the sales department has to let the customer know that quick lube is available during the introduction to the service department. Third, the service department should concentrate on quick lube during new-car clinics. Finally, the dealership needs an effective marketing plan to attract customers via mailers, digital marketing, and other channels.

It is a good idea to run a quick lube/express service as a stand-alone business with dedicated manager and staff. The main premise of quick lube is that a customer can drive in without an appointment and get an oil change done within forty-five minutes. A dedicated manager will ensure proper staffing levels, attentive customer service, and most importantly, increased revenue through up-sell. It is critical to treat the customers right since they are much more likely to come back for much more profitable maintenance and repair work.

A lot of dealers are caught up with an idea that if they change the oil in fifteen minutes or less, they are doing a great job. The point is not to rush through the process but to maximize revenue by up-selling items such as air filters, wiper blades, light bulbs, belts, and cabin filters. To ensure maximum up-sell opportunity, an A-skilled tech should oversee the work of lube technicians. Low-skill techs performing oil changes in most quick lube/express service locations do not have the necessary experience to diagnose a problem.

Many dealers do not take advantage of converting quick lube/express service customers into sales customers. There needs to be a process to identify high-mileage cars and offer customers to trade in their cars. The bottom line is that running an effective quick-lube operation allows a dealership to increase customer satisfaction and retention, as well as customer-paid labor and sales of new and used cars.

Warranty Administration
Warranty administration is an important aspect of a successful service department. Dealers can either outsource this work or do it themselves, in-house. I strongly suggest using a third party because they will only get paid if you get paid, so there is an obvious incentive. However you choose to do it, I recommend using scanning software to simplify the audit process and avoid chargebacks. It is not a bad idea to have a paperless environment in the twenty-first century. It will save you time, space, and aggravation.

Waiting Area

The Perfect Dealership must provide a convenient waiting area for its service customers. Snacks, coffee, and soft drinks must be provided. I strongly recommend providing a business center, so customers can conduct their business while they are waiting for the car. It is also important to provide loaners and shuttles to retain customers. As I said before, customers are willing to pay more for good service and convenience. You will attract the better breed, as well.

Service Retention Programs

Service managers should encourage the sales manager to either give away or sell at high-penetration rates prepaid maintenance. Prepaid maintenance guarantees a flow of customers coming back to the service department. This flow of customers will you're your dealership during the next economic downturn. These visits allow service advisors to build relationships with customers and eventually up-sell them the necessary maintenance/repair work. The idea is to lure the customer in, not with smoke and mirrors or questionable promise and shenanigans but with genuinely good service and deals and then to build on these. Another option is to offer an engine-for-life guarantee. Basically, the dealership guarantees the engine for as long as the customer owns the car as long as the customer performs the scheduled maintenance at the dealership's service department. This approach creates a separation from competition for the sales department and increases service retention. In addition, it is a good idea to set up a loyalty program, so customers can accumulate points for every dollar spent in the service and parts department. Customers are very familiar with loyalty programs and will appreciate it.

Third-Party Service Contracts and Ancillary Products

The service department must be well versed in filing claims with third-party service contract providers. Service advisors must work closely with the F&I department to know what third-party service contracts and ancillary products are being sold and how to quickly file a claim.

Service advisors should be offering service contracts to customers whose factory warranty is over or about to expire. This can be accomplished through additional sales training and closely working with the F&I department.

Recruitment

It is becoming harder and harder to find qualified technicians. The best approach is to develop talent internally. In order to do that, the Perfect Dealership develops relationships with local technical schools, hires graduates, and gives them the path to becoming A techs. The service manager must develop a training program for the new hires.

Unsold Customer Follow-Up

Whenever customers decline work to be done on their car, a declination line should be added to the repair order. Later, either BDC staff or service advisors should contact these customers and remind them to do the declined work.

Chapter Eight

F & I

Why We Do F&I—Arrange Financing and Provide Products

Your F&I department is a true profit center, especially considering how compressed front-end margins are in the current market, and this margin will only get tighter as the bigger Internet players make their moves. F&I departments, if not run properly, can get the dealership in trouble, both financially and when it comes to compliance. If well run, recent reports state they can generate as much as 47 percent of total profits.

Lack of Training

F&I managers are highly paid professionals that in most cases lack professional training. As I said before, there is no major at a local university for key positions in our field. The Perfect Dealership invests in the training of our finance managers on an ongoing basis. Product knowledge and sales training is a must, particularly for a department with such profit-generating potential. Unfortunately, a lot of finance managers couldn't answer basic product-knowledge questions such as whether consequential damage is covered under the terms of the service contract.

Certification/Compliance

Large publicly held auto groups (AutoNation, Group 1, Asbery, et al.) report F&I profits ranging from $1,200 to over $1,500 per retailed unit. In the current environment, F&I is a true profit center for any successful dealership. In fact, the possibilities are rich, but it is easy to get carried away with payment packing and F&I product jamming without proper compliance and internal controls.

In many instances, illegal or unethical practices of F&I managers trigger investigations by federal and state regulatory agencies. Such investigations are of a scale that they sometimes make the news, and in these cases it is an uphill battle to repair a dealer's reputation.

That is, we are currently experiencing proactive regulators who go after car dealers at high rates. This is due to three factors: (1) car dealers do not have the best reputation (2) going after car dealers generates headlines that in turn can further the career of a particular attorney general or an investigator, and (3) more importantly, retail sales are at their highest levels, and regulators are in a solid position to collect large fines and penalties.

Practical Steps to Having a Compliant F&I Department

Every dealer should start by appointing a compliance officer and giving that person the necessary authority to enforce corporate policy and procedure as well as to conduct the required training. The compliance officer must oversee the finance department and check deal folders, listen to audio (if available), and watch the video interactions of all finance managers and customers. Good management requires vigilance. There is a way to be fair as you quietly monitor all operations around you. Unfortunately, you'll need to incorporate a certain amount of fear into the process—simply by making your F&I people aware of these controls—to keep things level.

In keeping with what they can generate, finance managers are highly paid professionals—$250,000 a year is not inordinate and is commensurate with an old Wall Street salary. At the same time, the talent pool is pretty shallow, and dealers must make sure that they are getting the best candidates to fill the position. The first and most important step will be to conduct a background check and a drug test. The background check should also include a criminal and a credit check. As mentioned before, it is a good idea to test for prescription drugs. The second step is to actually check the candidates' references. I wouldn't just call previous employers as it is not as effective as calling lenders that dealt with the applicant. Lending sources will tell if the candidate submitted clean deals and if there were any issues like power booking and credit application falsification.

Unfortunately for the auto industry, there is very limited professional training for this work. Again, there is no degree in F&I at a local university, so, in most cases, it is on-the-job training plus the sales training provided by F&I vendors. I personally have much experience in this area. We encourage all of our dealers to employ finance managers who have successfully completed AFIP certification. AFIP stands for the Association for Finance and Insurance Professionals. AFIP certification helps finance managers learn federal and state laws that govern F&I, just as it helps them to adhere to an established code of ethics. Dealers should either hire AFIP-certified professionals or demand that their existing finance managers obtain this certification. Moreover, there are regular courses provided by your local dealer association, and dealers should take advantage of this training and send their finance managers to these courses on a regular basis.

The third step is to have a clearly defined policy and procedure. An effective onboarding process for any new hire must follow this. Total Dealer Compliance helps dealers design effective policy and procedures, and our online courses are an excellent way to familiarize finance managers with relevant regulations.

The fourth step is to establish a fair credit–compliance program that outlines the dealer participation rate. This program is designed to prevent disparate impact and explains predetermined allowable deviations. Predetermined deviations include the following:

- participation limited by a lender
- customer has monthly payment constraint
- competitive offer
- dealership promotional financing campaign
- manufacturer subvention program
- dealership employee incentive program
- dealership inventory reduction consideration

(These deviations must be documented and filed in a deal folder.)

The next area of vulnerability in the F&I department is the sale of ancillary products such as service contracts, tire and wheel protection, lease wear and tear, paint and fabric protection, and so forth. There should be a uniform pricing for all the products offered in F&I department to avoid being accused of discrimination. Similar to rate participation, deviations from the uniform pricing must be documented and filed in the deal folder.

F&I Product/Vendor Assessment
It is important to vet F&I products to make sure that these products are approved by state insurance departments and that they are properly underwritten. Moreover, we see that F&I vendors are solely responsible for the training of finance managers as well as F&I compliance. There is an inherent conflict of interest since F&I providers make money through sales of F&I products and might look the other way when it comes to noncompliant behavior or practices. At the very minimum, we recommend that F&I providers be AFIP certified. Not to muddy the water in the least, the best practice is to employ an independent compliance auditor to ensure adherence to the relevant rules and regulations.

Realistic F&I Profit Expectations
Dealer principals are often guilty of having unrealistic sales and profit expectations. If there is a $2,500 back-end profit expectation, I can tell you with a 100 percent certainty that there will be complaints, cancellations, investigations, newspaper headlines, and huge fines—in that particular order. The Perfect Dealership knows what the realistic industry KPIs (Key Performance Indicator) are and doesn't pressure finance managers to engage in unethical/noncompliant behavior to achieve inflated numbers.

To Summarize

Nationwide auto retail sales are at the highest levels, and dealers are targets of investigations by state and federal agencies. Do whatever it takes to help your dealership preserve this income. To ensure a compliant F&I department, several factors must be present:

- background checks, drug tests, and references
- certification and ongoing training
- effective policy, procedures, and onboarding process
- F&I product and vendor assessment
- clearly defined product penetration requirements and profit expectations

Menu Presentation

The finance department is tasked with obtaining the most favorable financing options for the customer as well as maximizing profitability by selling F&I products. A lot of times I see that there is no uniform process when it comes to this critical profit center. Dealers rely on the best efforts of their finance managers instead of focusing on standardized process and performance benchmarks. Product penetration percentages and PVR (Per Vehicle Retailed) are not mentioned in the job descriptions, and a lot of times, dealers hope for the best. Menu selling is the most effective tool when properly used to make sure that 100 percent of products are presented 100 percent of the time to 100 percent of the customers. Most sophisticated dealers use electronic menus that integrate with DMS software; however, installing a menu system is not enough. It is absolutely critical to implement effective policies and procedures in order to obtain a desired outcome. Below are the most effective policies and procedures using the DMAIC process. DMAIC is the core tool used in Six Sigma projects.

- Define the objective—the dealer principal or general manager must state what the desired PVR and product penetration percentage are.
- Measure—start by measuring the last twelve months of production in order to account for seasonal changes.
- Analyze—assess what products are being sold, as well as the average gross profit and penetration for each product.
- Improve—set a desired PVR and product penetration, and train finance managers on how to effectively present the menu. Implement a pay plan that incentivizes finance managers to perform at the optimum level.
- Control—review and incrementally increase desired outcome on a monthly or quarterly basis.

It is essential that there is a fail-safe mechanism to make sure that finance managers are using the menu. I recommend not to bill a deal unless there is a signed menu. Another approach is to use a menu that monitors the key strokes; this way, the dealer will know how much time the finance manager spent presenting each product. Following these steps will allow the finance department to increase product penetration and gross profit while increasing customer retention.

Displaying F&I Products on the Dealer Website
If you look at dealership websites, you will see that they offer a lot of information. For example, you can research cars, make service appointments, and get an appraisal on a trade-in.

Almost never will you see any information about service contracts or ancillary products that the dealership sells in its F&I department.

This needs to change as the consumers demand and expect more transparency. Moreover, providing information about F&I products will speed up the F&I process in the dealership and increase customer satisfaction with the buying process.

As online car buying is perfected, there will be a need to develop online presentation for each and every F&I product being sold. Dealers need to start preparing and implementing these presentations as soon as possible. This is an inevitable change. Properly presented F&I products will sell themselves.

Working Together with Service Department

As mentioned in the service and parts chapter (chapter 7), the service department must work together with the F&I department to know what products are being sold and how to file a claim. Regular meetings should be held between your service and parts director and your director of finance. If service advisors do not know how to file a claim or do not want to be bothered with third-party service contracts and ancillary products, your finance department will lose credibility, and it will only be harder to sell these products in the future.

Reinsurance

I am amazed at how many dealers are not reinsuring their service contract business as well as some of their ancillary products. Reinsurance is an excellent source of income as well as a great tax strategy. Reinsurance allows a dealer to earn underwriting profits plus any investment income that is earned on these premiums.

Re-insurance programs are not created equal so do the necessary research. Pay attention to the administration fee as well as ceding and loss adjustment fee.

A great strategy is to create white-label service contracts and white-label ancillary products.

This approach helps increase customer service and retention. More importantly, it is an excellent way to improve branding at your dealership.

Tie-Back and Disappearing Deductible
Tie-back is another excellent strategy. Tie-back requires customers to come back to the selling dealer service department for all repairs as long as the breakdown is within a predefined radius—typically within fifty or seventy-five miles of the selling dealership.

This approach is great way to control claims and load the dealer's shop.

A "disappearing deductible" is another great strategy to ensure that customers come back to the selling dealer service department. Basically, there is a $0 deductible if the customer comes back to the selling dealer versus a $200 or $300 deductible if the customer goes somewhere else.

Finance managers that have excellent product knowledge will be able to explain to the customer the beauty of a disappearing deductible.

Preload Programs to Enhance Your "Why Buy from Us" Story

In order to improve your dealership's bottom line and remain relevant in the digital age, it is important to consider two main factors: how to set yourself apart from the competition, and where to specifically focus on increasing profit margins.

When devising a solid strategy to accomplish these objectives, it's crucial to identify universal trends in consumers' retail preferences and align your dealership's sales techniques appropriately. Management must also continually think outside of the box to come up with tactics that position its salespeople most optimally in the eyes of their customers.

The Value of Preinstalled Add-Ons

This is not an easy task, but to be successful, every dealership must find a way to address and conquer these challenges. One way to achieve increased income is by preinstalling low-cost items that are perceived by consumers as high value and positioning them as complimentary add-ons. These items include

- dealer-branded prepaid maintenance, which guarantees a customer will come back to the selling dealer's service department to perform scheduled maintenance. What's more, this maintenance plan can only be used at the selling dealer, unlike OEM prepaid maintenance, which can be used at any dealership;

- exterior paint protection, which helps keep the car looking new and increases its trade-in value; and
- antitheft protection, which is valuable because car theft is still a prevalent crime in many areas.

The Importance of Up-Selling

Additionally, to offset the cost of the preload, a dealership's F&I department must be able to up-sell the exterior paint protection and prepaid maintenance to longer terms and antitheft protection to a greater dollar amount. To do so, a dealership's senior management team should set a certain up-sell penetration requirement to incentivize its sales teams.

Adding these items to an overall comprehensive sales strategy will undoubtedly create a sense of loyalty, cultivate a more positive opinion of the dealership, and improve profit margins.

Draw Attention to the Add-Ons

Dealers should also be sure to prominently display the items they are including in the sale price of the car on a separate addendum sticker. Sales staff should be trained accordingly and fully understand the value added by the products to vehicles to better position them with customers.

The information featured on the addendum stickers should also be included in a dealership's print and online efforts (website, TV, radio, Internet, and social media). There should also be marketing materials on every salesperson's desk to reinforce the message.

Dealerships cannot implement a one-size-fits-all approach, however. The items mentioned here are just a few examples of the types of innovations that dealerships must implement in order to stay competitive in the ever-changing marketplace. With dealerships rushing to stand out, many implement tactics without properly validating their customers' needs first, leading to hit-or-miss results. By focusing on benefits as universal as these added perks and low-cost items, dealerships eliminate any risk of failure.

Often the car sales process begins online, but there is still a strong need for brick-and-mortar auto dealerships. By showcasing new, innovative ways to stay competitive, dealerships can adapt to changing customer needs and improve their bottom line. It is a good idea to reinsure the preloaded products because of tax advantages and reduction in commissionable gross profit.

Prepaid Maintenance
We briefly discussed prepaid maintenance in the parts and service chapter (chapter 7). Prepaid maintenance guarantees a flow of customers coming back to the service department. These visits allow service advisors to build relationships with customers and eventually up-sell them the necessary maintenance and repair work.

Now, let's look at prepaid maintenance from the income-development perspective. There are two types of prepaid maintenance that dealers offer: OEM or their own. The Perfect Dealership only offers its own prepaid maintenance.

First, let's examine OEM offering. OEM maintenance comes from the manufacturer and is good at any dealership. For example, if you sell Honda maintenance, your customers can use it at any Honda dealership in the United States.

Now, if the customer doesn't use prepaid maintenance, then breakage is kept by the OEM and becomes their profit, meaning the premium that your dealership paid for prepaid maintenance is kept by the manufacturer if the customer doesn't use it.

Let's take a closer look at the dealer-owned prepaid maintenance. The dealer designs the program and hires a third party to administer it. The main advantages of this approach are as follows:

First, customers can only use the prepaid maintenance at the selling dealership, therefore increasing service retention. Second, customers are actively contacted to make sure that they come to redeem their services. Good program administrators can increase customer retention up to 75 percent. This allows service advisers to build relationship with customers and eventually upsell required maintenance and repair work. Third, the breakage is returned to the dealer and becomes additional profit.

Smooth Cancellation Process

Oftentimes customers need to cancel F&I products they bought, and the cancellation process in many dealerships is not the greatest. These dealerships are guilty of giving the customer a runaround, and that's unacceptable. In most cases, if these products were properly presented and explained, there would be no need to cancel them. There must be a written cancellation/refund process, and every finance manager has to follow it. Better yet let the compliance officer oversee the cancellation process.

Lender Relationships

Indirect lending is a huge part of a dealership's operations. It is paramount to maintain good relationships with lenders and have a diversified portfolio of banks interested in doing business with your dealerships.

Often, I see that finance managers are not really familiar with the subprime part of the business and shy away from it completely. The finance director should work closely with subprime bank reps to make sure that his or her department is maximizing every opportunity and fulfilling its mission of arranging financing for all customers.

Choosing a Right F&I Vendor

Every dealership works with an F&I vendor, and I want to dedicate this section to choosing the right one. The F&I vendor should be an integral part of a successful finance department.

There are three types of F&I vendors—big box companies such as JM&A and Zurich, smaller independent general agents, and OEM. Companies such as JM&A and Zurich put up one hell of a presentation when they fly in six guys in suits. Unfortunately, you won't see them ever again. Dealers end up being serviced by inexperienced account reps who usually get promoted or reassigned to a different territory. There is no continuity of substance in this masquerade. And that's not to mention the sky-high admin fees.

Smaller independent agents also fall into two categories. The first category is what I called "accidental agents." They became agents by accident because they are friends with the dealer principal. In most cases, these guys have never worked in the car business and really don't understand it. Therefore, they can't provide quality training or bring income-development ideas to the table. The only thing they are good at is wining and dining the dealer.

The second category is a tiny minority, but these guys really know what they are doing, and working with them can make a huge difference. They have prior dealership experience as GMs or directors of finance and understand the business. They will provide quality training, set benchmarks and hold finance managers accountable, and bring excellent income-development solutions as well as help the dealership implement them.

I strongly suggest that dealer principals really examine and assess who their F&I vendors are and what they do for them.

OEMs such as Nissan recognize that F&I is a great way to generate additional revenue, and they aggressively market F&I products to their dealers. OEMs incentivize dealers through additional trunk money and reduced interest rates on the floor plan. I have been doing F&I consulting for many years and can say with 100 percent certainty that OEMs do not have the necessary expertise. F&I is not just about products but training and motivating. Third-party solutions coupled with an effective general agent will always produce better results.

Follow-Up with Unsold F&I Customers
I rarely (almost never) see a dealership where there is a defined process of following up with customers who declined to purchase F&I products at the time of delivery.

It is not uncommon for customers to not buy products, and dealers should follow up at a later time to try again. This strategy is guaranteed to increase product penetration. The dealership has to decide whether finance managers or BDC staff will do this follow up.

Conclusion

F&I is an extremely important department, and it is paramount to hire the right people, train them, and set realistic expectations. In addition, F&I is where dealers make a lion's share of their money. The Perfect Dealership uses a menu, reinsures F&I products, and has multiple preloads. It is important to understand that the F&I department if not properly run can cause tremendous losses (financial and reputational) through noncompliant and unethical practices. The Perfect Dealership employs a compliance officer and has strong internal controls.

Chapter Nine

IT

On the Internet, simplicity rules. I mean this in both the informational and transactional sense. I still see many dealer websites that are confusing, hard to use, or lacking in the necessary functionality. More and more people conduct their daily business online, and dealers need to take a closer look at their online assets.

The Perfect Dealership keeps up with the latest website technologies, with its competitors, and also with what leading Internet retailers are doing.

It is a good idea to look frequently at Amazon.com, Uber, Vroom. com, and so forth. Each is extremely user friendly and engaging. It is a tribute to Amazon's organizational ability that their interface does not appear to change that much. They simply add other rooms and dimensions, so to speak, to a structure that works. It is seamless; you learn it once and don't struggle with it. (They are a superb company, the main apex predator moving into our arena already, right now, beginning first in Europe with Fiat.)

Simply put, dealers should consider redesigning their websites with the same attention they apply in redesigning their showrooms. In the near future, more and more business will be conducted online, and dealers need to do whatever it takes to keep up with changing trends and buying habits. And yet the key continuities are already evident, such as the need for transparency with the educated consumer, who has all comparative data at his or her fingertips. As stated in earlier chapters, transparency is no longer something to be considered as an option; it is a necessity now carved in stone.

Currently, customers can research a vehicle, book a service appointment, and even buy parts online on the dealership website. What they cannot do in 99 percent of the cases is research F&I products and buy a car online. At the very minimum, they should be able to complete as much of the buying process as possible online before going to the showroom to pick up their car.

Treat your website and IT infrastructure like a precious piece of real estate that will make you a living. This is in fact what it has become. Remember that the Perfect Dealership is open twenty-four hours like Amazon.com. Pay attention to every little detail, every webpage. I urge all dealers to have a detailed (with contact information and pictures) Meet the Staff page. This way customers know who to contact if they have a question or concern. Missing pictures on Meet the Staff page is unprofessional and customers pay attention.

It is worth noting that most customers use their smartphones to visit websites so it is mission critical to have an easy-to-navigate, functioning mobile site. Also, research various color schemes because customers react differently to various colors. For example, a majority of people interpret blue as solid and reliable. No wonder that Goldman Sachs's website is dominated by a blue color scheme.

Now let's talk about computers that dealership employees use. I am amazed at how often I see desktops that are five or ten years old. It is important to update technology on a regular basis. Don't forget that due to the high speed of innovation, technology becomes obsolete quickly. We upgrade our smartphones every one or two years; let's do the same for our computers, servers, firewalls, routers, and so forth.

Lead Capture Should Integrate with CRM

Lead capture must integrate with CRM to effectively follow up with 100 percent of leads. And a service appointment scheduler should also integrate with CRM.

Make a single person accountable for each of these, and hold him or her to it. This is a good principle—accountability down to a person—that will save you from incoherence in your operations.

The Internet offers endless visual experience at the touch of buttons. Display multiple actual photos, never stock photos (which are usually meaningless to a client and suggest that you value expedience, at his or her expense). Inventory merchandising is critical in the Internet age. I repeat, stop using stock photos! Customers need to see the actual cars. Don't be afraid to take as many as forty pictures per vehicle.

Video Walk-Arounds Are Mandatory

In this day and age there is a need for video walk-arounds, of both new and used cars. Customers want information on demand, and the dealership that provides the most data in the easiest fashion will win the customer. This, again, is related to transparency. You go the extra mile to inform in every possible sense. This projects honesty, also. Conversely, anything that suggests sleight-of-hand or corner-cutting will be detrimental.

Trade-In Appraisal Tool

Here is a real opportunity to stand out and win over the customer. Perfect Dealerships must provide an accurate appraisal value for the customer's trade-in. It is a good idea to utilize a third-party tool such as Edmunds.com because of consumers' trust. Consumers don't trust the numbers that are put on cars by used car managers.

Find the tool that works the best for your sales process, and install the widget on your website. Customers do not want to hear, "Bring your car to the dealership, and our used car manager will put a number on it." They need this information on demand, and the appraisal needs to be concrete. With a concrete number in mind, the customer can focus and act. If customers are already on your website seeking information, give it! Then, lead them all the way through the sale. I cannot emphasize this enough. Make the experience seamless and simple. Think of your site or applications as your vital partner—a mechanized member of the dealership who knows absolutely everything, including clarity and decorum and how to approach every situation.

Again, the dealer with the most transparent and user-friendly sales process will win the war.

Conduct Sales Transactions Online Whenever Possible

As mentioned above, our buying habits are changing, and dealers need to keep up with these changes. Transactional websites are the future, whether you like it or not. Dealers need to make the decision on whether they will develop their own transactional websites or let third parties inject themselves between the customer and the dealer—similar to what Cars.com, Autotrader.com, and CarGurus.com did in the area of lead generation.

An important aside: There are battles raging in other industries that can inform you of some of the conflicts that can arise when you outsource or begin to rely on third parties. Admittedly, this can be hard to avoid, especially if technology has been the instigator. Study the recent moves by Streeteasy.com, a third-party middleman that has just acted to further profit from the real estate listings market in New York City, at the expense of the top brokerages—read, dealerships—that once monopolized this market. Streeteasy just imposed a $6-a-day fee per rental listing on the brokerages. This works out to $180 per month per apartment. If an agent has five listings, this could cost the brokerage or the agent close to $1,000 a month. As of this writing, the gloves are off, and the top brokerages are struggling against a listings-only website. Streeteasy is not customer-facing but wants to position itself between the brokers and their buyers—in the business these brokers once ruled.

Digital retailing is a must for a Perfect Dealership. Most dealers are afraid of the transparency that digital retail represents because they fear a decrease in profits. Lower margins are inevitable, but what a Perfect Dealership gets in return is expanded market share and reduced employee compensation.

Booking Service Appointments

As discussed in the chapter on parts and service, it is important to utilize shop-loading software when booking service appointments online or on the phone. Perfect Dealerships also allow their customers to request a loaner at the time of booking an appointment. The loaner is a critical part of a seamless, satisfying experience for customers, who should be accommodated when their own cars are being fixed.

Computer Security

Computer security is paramount in today's business environment. Dealers need to hire network engineers with computer security credentials. It is critical to protect customer data. In case of a data breach, most customers will not go back to that dealer to buy another car. Beware of outsourcing this to the lowest possible bidder (for example, a service provider in a foreign country). You may want to do this with a reputable US firm.

The chances of getting hit are not remote. There are numerous examples of companies such as Yahoo, eBay, and JP Morgan Chase being hacked. There is a steady illegal, online business in identity theft and the selling of your clients' personal financial data. Dealers should purchase cyber liability and data breach insurance and have a protocol in place in case of a hack.

Educating employees in computer security is a must and needs to be done during onboarding for new hires and throughout the year for existing employees. Employees should know what files they can and cannot download. It is a good idea to limit websites that employees can browse to reduce the probability of downloading a virus and to increase productivity.

E-mail Policy and Social Media Policy

Your employee handbook should have a clearly defined e-mail policy. It is a good idea to install software that checks every outgoing e-mail. For example, if the software detects a sequence of numbers (Social Security numbers or credit card numbers), it will prevent the e-mail from going out and will alert your network administrator to investigate.

The employee handbook should also have a clearly defined social media policy. Employees need to know what they can and cannot post on their social networks. For example, it is not a good idea to have salespeople advertise cars inside their own social networks unless all the necessary disclosures are in place.

Full-Time Network Engineer

In the early days of the Internet, it was OK to have a part-time staff or to completely outsource IT functions. Now, it is mission critical to have a full-time network administrator. You can't afford to have your network go down for a minute. This is one of the worst impressions a customer can receive: "This site is down temporarily." Nothing appears to be weaker these days than a business that cannot stay online. This is something that sticks negatively in all of our minds when we encounter it, because it suggests site vulnerability or, at least, poor technical prowess. In addition, computer security is a never-ending task.

Be on a Constant Lookout for Technical Innovations

The perfect dealer is on the lookout for technical innovations and is not afraid to invest in technology. Today's climate is about leading, not waiting until you are forced to do something smart.

Again, think long term. Once you start to see a return on this kind of investment—technical innovation with leading-edge performance—you will be sold on both the sense of leadership and feeling of greater confidence in your own abilities that it instills. This is important and a solid move against your worst enemy: inertia. When you are proactive and strive to become technically innovative in what is now a "techno-tronic" age, you have moved apart from the old dealership paradigm. This would be one of the more important steps into the new terrain this book is concerned with.

Develop a Dealer App
A dealer app is a must-have for any dealer. Customers use their smartphones 24-7, and having a dealer app downloaded is the most valuable real estate in the electronic age. Work to perfect this app just as you would a new BDC software, for example. The identity of the dealership is a hybrid of human and machine now, as it has always been with cars as the product. But the computer and the programs you create to try to perfect your dealership are as essential now to your operations as computerized components are to the ongoing, excellent engineering in the vehicles you sell.

Further, your dealer app should utilize push notifications. These are an effective way to communicate with customers, especially as more and more promotional e-mails are going into spam or getting deleted before being read.

Of course, your dealer app needs to provide all the necessary functionality: appointment scheduler, test-drive scheduler, user manual, loyalty program, and so forth. There are companies that specialize in dealer app development, so the dealer doesn't have to make a huge investment.

Do Whatever It Takes to Prevent a Data Breach

Dealerships are treasure troves of customer nonpublic information, and dealers must do whatever it takes to protect it. That means focusing on both physical and electronic security. All too often I see offices without doors or without locks. My favorite is the when there is a lock but no key.

Total Dealer Compliance conducted a study, and here is what we found:

- Just under 84 percent of consumers will not go back to buy another vehicle from a dealership after their data has been compromised.
- More than 70 percent of dealers are not up to date on their antivirus software.
- Only 30 percent of dealers employ a network engineer with computer security certifications/training.
- Only 25 percent hired a third-party vendor to try to hack into their networks to test their vulnerability.

Perfect Dealerships hire a third party to try to break into their own network to assess its vulnerability. This is absolutely necessary to objectively determine the level of preparedness. There are several reputable white-hat hackers who provide these types of services. In case the breach happens, a dealership needs to have a data-breach protocol in place in order to effectively communicate with customers, law enforcement agencies, the media, and network engineers.

Chapter Ten

Ten Commandments

The car business is an amazing business and can be very fulfilling. I truly hope that this book will help make it better for both dealers and customers. The main takeaways I want you to remember from this book are the following:

1. Remember, automotive retail is a career, not a temporary gig.
2. Have a customer-centric approach behind every decision.
3. Focus on employee development that provides a path for career growth.
4. Have a clearly defined mission statement and organizational goals shared by all departments.
5. Develop a compliance and ethics program, as it is the bloodline for longevity.
6. Adopt the latest technology to simplify the sales process.
7. Identify and develop profit centers.

8. Focus on customer retention more than on customer acquisition.
9. Engage in effective public relations and marketing to improve reputation and sales.
10. Attract a better workforce through improved pay plans, schedules, and training.

I wrote this book because I don't want car business to be the next Blockbuster. Dealer principals, general managers, and dealership employees need to adopt and change in order to survive the digital disruption. Doing business the old way is no longer an option.

I would love to hear your thoughts, answer your questions, and exchange ideas so please reach out to me at max@maxzanan. com. Also, visit www.PerfectDealership.com where I post new ideas, strategies, and solutions on how to improve customer experience and the dealership's bottom line.

Made in the USA
Monee, IL
02 January 2020